W9-CDC-660

and twelve. Included are many ready-to-teach units of study, designed to develop an awareness of the world of work in the primary grades; narrow the student's focus, based on realistic self-appraisal, in junior high and early high school; and prepare students for a vocation or higher education in grades eleven and twelve.

Based on fifteen career clusters developed by the U.S. Office of Education, the suggested curriculum also includes worksheets, questionnaires, statistics, activities, lessons and techniques for teaching.

What's more, the curriculum comes with reports from various school systems—large and small, rural, suburban and urban—which are now implementing their own programs.

Plus, there are extensive listings enabling you to send for a virtual library of career education information.

You'll be hard-pressed to find as much solid, practical information on career education in one handy guide. It's a complete package—invaluable help to guarantee that your students' awakening to the world of work will *not* be a rude one.

ABOUT THE AUTHOR

MURIEL SCHOENBRUN KARLIN is a Supervisor of the Board of Education of the City of New York, and writes the weekly column "Making It," an educational and vocational guidance report in the *Staten Island Advance*. In addition, she is editor of Parker's monthly publication, the *Career Education Workshop*. With extensive experience in teaching, educational and vocational guidance, and teacher training, Mrs. Karlin is also Assistant Principal in charge of career education and language arts at a New York City junior high school. She has contributed many articles to educational journals, and has a prodigious number of books to her credit: *Solving Your Career Mystery; Pathways to Careers* (with co-author Morton Margules); and (with co-author Regina Berger) *Individualizing Instruction: A Complete Guide for Diagnosis, Planning, Teaching and Evaluation; Discipline and the Disruptive Child: A Practical Guide for Elementary Teachers; The Effective Student Activities Program; Experiential Learning; An Effective Teaching Program for the Elementary School;* and *Successful Methods for Teaching the Slow Learner.*

Administrator's Guide
to a Practical
Career Education
Program

Other Books Authored by Muriel Karlin and Regina Berger

Successful Methods for Teaching the Slow Learner
The Effective Student Activities Program
Discipline and the Disruptive Child: A Practical Guide for Elementary Teachers
Experiential Learning: An Effective Teaching Program for Elementary Schools
Individualized Learning: Complete Guide for Planning, Teaching and Evaluation

Administrator's Guide to a Practical Career Education Program

*Muriel
Schoenbrun
Karlin*

BRIAR CLIFF COLLEGE
LIBRARY

SIOUX CITY, IOWA

Parker Publishing Company, Inc.   West Nyack, New York

© 1974 by
PARKER PUBLISHING COMPANY, INC.
West Nyack, New York

*All rights reserved. No part of this book
may be reproduced in any form or by any
means, without permission in writing from
the publisher.*

LC
1047.8
.K37

Library of Congress Cataloging in Publication Data

Karlin, Muriel Schoenbrun.
    Administrator's guide to a practical career educa-
tion program.

    Bibliography: p.
    1. Vocational education--Administration. 2. Voca-
tional guidance. I. Title.
LC1047.8.K37   370.11'3   74-11482
ISBN 0-13-005025-3

Printed in the United States of America

To Len, Lisa and Henry

72495

How This Book Will Help You, The Professional Educator

There is no question that career education has been sadly neglected in the past. We have taught such subjects as algebra, but not how to use it to earn a living . . . some students do not even know what education is required to become a teacher . . . and other students in elementary or secondary school say they would like to go on to college, but haven't the vaguest notion of what courses or goals to aim for. Many children do not even have an accurate idea of what their fathers and mothers do to earn a living. Career education is one of those subject areas where it was felt that "we really ought to do something," but, all too often, we didn't.

In some schools, courses in occupations have been given for a year or two—rarely for more. The detailed program you will find in these pages, however, differs greatly from the standard course in occupations. It is a comprehensive and *practical* program—one that can cover the formative years of the student's school life. It can easily be adjusted to take up less time in the beginning and expanded as the program proves its value.

Career education involves developing a child's awareness of the world of work in grades K through 6 (Chapters 7, 8 and 9) through a study of the fifteen career clusters into which the world of work has been divided. In grades 7 through 9 (Chapter 10) he studies three of these clusters in detail, and selects a possible entry-level job from one of the three. In grade ten he is taught the skills necessary for that job. In grades eleven and twelve (Chapter 11) he may do either of the following: prepare for work by learning more skills, or proceed toward post high school education in a precollege program.

This program helps to insure that no young adult will graduate from high school without, at least, the key skills that will enable him to find employment.

In each of the following chapters you will find realistic techniques, methods, concepts and ideas—all given with the utmost practicality in mind. The book is divided into two parts. Part One discusses the establishment of the Career Education Program, and Part Two gives specific curricula. The first chapter underscores the acute need for the program so that you have the selling points, should you need to sell it. You are shown how to establish specific goals for your program—goals that take into consideration the socio-economic as well as the intellectual environment in which each child lives. Plans are included for gaining acceptance for the Career Education Program from your school board, your parents, and your community. Chapter 3 will help you decide which form your program should take, with a number of realistic alternatives to be considered.

Any program can succeed or fail depending on the actual teaching. With this in mind, Chapter 4 includes specific ways to develop an extensive awareness and skills program that the teachers will enjoy and in which they will become involved. Motivating the student is of critical importance, and methods that have been used successfully are included in Chapter 5.

A Career Education Program can draw value from many sources. These will be listed, with suggestions for their effective use. A central location, such as a media center, can be highly effective, but is not essential. If you do not have the funds or the facilities, there are excellent, inexpensive alternatives.

Career education is vital education. Your program should be adjusted to help meet the needs of the community so that, at the same time, you will be meeting the needs of the students. Specific techniques are included to help you do this. Every program needs constant evaluation, and the Career Education Program is no exception. In Chapter 6 you will find practical material which will help you measure your progress.

Part Two includes specific curricula that ranges from kindergarten through the twelfth grade. The basic concepts, techniques, model lesson plans, suggested uses for personnel, and course offerings are listed. The curricula are written with the teacher in mind so as to enable you to easily and quickly adapt them for your own administrative purposes.

In this book you will find realistic, practical material that will enable you, by working with your counselors and teachers, to establish a productive Career Education Program. Your counselors who have developed many skills in this field will be your key people, helping you to establish and operate the program successfully.

Students *need* an effective Career Education Program, and we believe your time and effort will be richly rewarded. Moreover, we are sure you will find the basis for instituting such a program in this book.

Muriel Schoenbrun Karlin

ACKNOWLEDGMENTS

Sincere thanks to the many people who helped in the preparation of this manuscript:

Mr. Norman H. Harris, Principal, Anning S. Prall Intermediate School, Staten Island, New York.

Superintendent Jerome G. Kovalcik, Office of Education Information Services and Public Relations, Board of Education, City of New York.

Secretary of Education Sidney Marland, Office of Education, Department of Health, Education and Welfare, Washington, D.C.

Mr. Philip J. Stella, Director/Producer Channel 7 ITV, Normandy High School, Parma, Ohio.

Dr. Lawrence Costello, Principal, August Martin High School, Queens, New York.

Superintendent Oral W. Spurgeon, Special School District of Saint Louis County, Rock Hill, Missouri.

Superintendent T.C. Porter, Nelsonville, Ohio.

Dr. Robert Schrader, Superintendent of Public Instruction, Cheyenne, Wyoming.

Mr. Max Benitz, Meredith Halliday and the staff of the Washington State Council for Occupational Education.

The entire staff of the Office of Education, Department of Health, Education and Welfare, Washington, D.C.

These and many other dedicated educators contributed information that has been included in these pages.

Special thanks to Mrs. Helen R. Harris, Educational and Vocational Counselor, Public School 82, Manhattan for her proofreading of the manuscript before publication; to Mrs. Irene Weiss, of Cedarhurst, New York, to Mrs. Brenda Smith of Manhattan, for their typing of the manuscript; to Miss Regina Berger, for her constant help and reinforcement; and to the Karlin family for their encouragement and assistance.

And, above all, my thanks to the children I am privileged to work with every day, who are, really, the source of inspiration for all of my writing, and to my readers, whose reactions have made all of the effort worthwhile.

M.S.K.

TABLE OF CONTENTS

Why do 2½ million young people have few, if any skills . . . Why are
13 million Americans supported by public assistance . . . The disappearing unskilled jobs . . . The lack of skilled workers . . . Connecting years of education with future income . . . Financing post
high school education . . . Establishing specific goals for your Career
Education Program . . . Helping develop self-awareness . . . Developing an understanding of the variety of careers possible . . . Compre-
hending what specific tasks each career entails . . . The career ladder
concept . . . Making every academic subject relevant to careers . . .
Connecting academic achievement in elementary, junior and senior
high schools with college . . . Making education meaningful to all
students . . . Understanding the economic facts of life . . . Young
women as well as young men need education in skills . . . Time and
money are needed for career training . . . Funds for every student . . . Careers by choice, not chance . . . Job satisfaction . . . Job
training for high school graduates . . . Academic preparation for
college . . . Training available throughout a person's life . . . What is
expected "on the job"? . . . The role of the guidance counselor in
Career Education . . . Going into business for oneself . . . Involving
faculty, parents, community members, and most of all students in
the Career Education Program.

The role of the superintendent of schools, the principal, and other
administrators in achieving this important curricular change . . . Special materials are forthcoming from the Office of Education, Department of Health, Education and Welfare . . . How to introduce the

program to the local school board . . . To the parents and community . . . Establishing a committee . . . The role of the counselors in the Career Education Program . . . Doing a follow up study of your graduates and former students. . . . How to develop a tentative program . . . Presenting this program–through meetings and conferences . . . Using the principal's newsletter to promote the program . . . Motivating the teachers . . . Teacher training . . . Using auxiliary personnel–aids, paraprofessionals, student assistants . . . Setting up workshops covering the day-to-day lessons for the entire curriculum . . . Conferences to discuss the program as it progresses . . . Using parents and members of the community as resource personnel . . . Setting up demonstration lessons . . . Inter-visitation . . . Team teaching . . . Making the program interesting.

3. Deciding the Form Your Career Education Program Will Take—Staffing It, and Suiting It to the Needs of Your Community 63

Establishing committees . . . The Career Education Research Committee . . . The Career Education Selection Committee . . . The ideal Career Education Program . . . In the elementary school . . . In the junior high school . . . In the senior high school for one, two, three or four years . . . Staffing will depend on budgetary allowances . . . Involving the people, the businesses, the institutions of the community in your program . . . Surveying the industries in the community to determine where the job opportunities are . . . The role of the United States Employment service in determining which career areas require trained personnel . . . Checking with professional organizations . . . Inviting representatives of businesses to speak . . . Arranging for visits to factories, stores, institutions . . . Surveying the neighboring communities for career opportunities . . . Surveying the nearest large cities for career opportunities . . . Civil service careers on city, state or federal levels . . . Using the information you have obtained to the greatest advantage.

4. How to Motivate and Train the Staff Involved in the Career Education Program 79

Teaching the staff to utilize the following techniques . . . The informal, group situation . . . Using trips to the greatest extent . . . Inviting parents or community members to speak to, or teach the class . . . Committee work . . . Individualizing instruction and working with each child . . . Use of the interview to learn about various careers . . . The correct use of printed materials as a basis for discussion . . . The use of audio-visual materials . . . Using programed learning . . . The use of closed circuit television in the Career Education Program . . . Doing Career Surveys . . .

The role of the guidance counselor in building the program . . . Guidance Materials . . . The Educator's Guide to Free Guidance Materials . . . The Occupational Outlook Handbook . . . The Occupational Outlook Quarterly . . . The United States Government Printing Office . . . B'nai Brith Vocational Service . . . Professional organizations . . . School published material . . . Civil Service Information for the Federal government . . . Civil Service Information in regard to your state and city . . . New York Life Insurance Company . . . Office of Education, Department of Health, Education and Welfare . . . College catalogs . . . Listing of Scholarships . . . The College Placement Annual . . . Newspaper and magazine articles . . . Old magazines . . . School produced materials . . . Electronic materials . . . Closed circuit television . . . Commercially available material . . . Human resources are most important; Developing a listing of parents and community members . . . Don't forget your staff when compiling your resources . . . Class and individual trips . . . The use of films and filmstrips.

Evaluation must be an on-going process . . . Basic steps in evaluation . . . Who should do the evaluation . . . Specific steps for the evaluation of career education . . . Teachers' evaluation form, in the elementary, intermediate or junior high school . . . Teacher's evaluation form for the high school . . . Pupil evaluation . . . Evaluation by other members of the staff . . . The Career Education Coordinator . . . Parent evaluation . . . Employer evaluation . . . Reviewing the results, and evaluating your program.

PART TWO: THE CURRICULUM

Developing Self-Awareness—Concepts and Understandings

Unit A: There is a dignity in all work people do.
Unit B: Every boy or girl will be able to choose a career.
Unit C: It is important to find a career one enjoys.
Unit D: What things do people need in order to live?
Unit E: Where do people get the things they need?
Unit F: What does the expression "earning a living" mean?

The Office of Education Approach
A Second Approach
A Third Alternate Approach

7th Grade

Unit A: Questionnaire for seventh graders.

Unit B:' Why do people work?

Unit C: Why should women as well as men plan for a career?

Unit D: Why should a person select a career cluster, rather than a specific career?

Unit E: What are the different levels of employment and how do they affect the salary a person earns?

Final Activities for each cluster
Culminating the year's work

8th grade

Unit A: Self-awareness of one's talents, strengths, abilities, and lack of abilities.

Unit B: Education and training for a career determines the career level.

Unit C: The career ladder concept.

Unit D: Financing one's education.

Unit E: The concept of the back-up career.

Doing Career Investigations

9th Grade

Unit A: Questionnaire: Where do your abilities, talents and interests lie?

Unit B: Clues to selecting a career.

Unit C: Following through—from selecting a career to being successful in it.

Unit D: Succeeding in high school and in post high education.

Unit E: Finding and getting started in that first job.

Doing Career Investigations

The need to begin at the beginning ... The selection of a skills course from a cluster area ... Courses meeting the needs of various communities ... The state of Washington and the fishing industry ... The Career Development Center in Dallas ... Parma, Ohio's Television Production and Broadcasting ... New York's Haaren High School's Mini Schools ... On-the-job Exploration and Training in Whittier, California ... The Special School District of St. Louis County, Missouri ... The Tri-County Joint Vocational High School

of Nelsonville, Ohio . . . Aviation and the August Martin High
School, Queens, N.Y. . . . The High School Internship Program . . .
Los Angeles Career Advisement . . . Xerox Learning Systems.

Administrator's Guide
to a Practical
Career Education
Program

PART ONE

The Basics of the
Career Education Program

1

Establishing
Specific Goals for the
Career Education Program

AIMS OF THE PROGRAM

According to the U.S. Office of Education, "There are more than 20,000 possible careers in America, diverse enough to encompass everyone's interests and abilities. Yet *2.5 million young people each year* graduate from or drop out of high school or college with no planned career and few if any marketable skills. It costs $28 billion dollars to 'educate' them for potential failure."

The statement continues: "Career Education is not a do-it-yourself kit that comes boxed, color-coded, and indexed. It is not a program so much as it is a concept to be adapted to the needs of each state or community."

First, let us define and briefly describe such a program as it is being carried on in the state of Washington, where it has been "in the works" since 1967. The group largely responsible for its development has been the Coordinating Council for Occupational Education. They define "career education" as follows:

> Career education is a term currently used to describe a sequentially developed education program offering career orientation, exploration, and job preparation for all students. Programs begin in the first grade, or earlier, and continue through adult life.

In the elementary school, children are informed about the wide range of occupations in our society, the role of each worker, and the interdependence of one job upon another. Special attention is given to the development of positive attitudes toward work. Students also learn about the general requirements for each occupation studied.

Junior high school students explore specific clusters of occupations through "hands on" types of experiences, observations in the field, and related classroom instruction. Assistance is provided in helping each student select an area for further specialization in the senior high school.

In the senior high school students pursue the occupational area they have selected. All students will exercise one of three options:

1. Intensive job preparation for entry into the world of work immediately upon graduating from high school.

2. Preparation for postsecondary occupational education.

3. Preparation for a four-year college or university.

Students preparing for postsecondary occupational education or four-year college programs continue to receive occupational cluster experiences, including work experience wherever and whenever this is possible. "Academic" subject areas are designed to relate to the professional area for which they are preparing. Students planning careers in specialized areas will be provided with basic skills in academic subjects which will further qualify them for advanced study in their selected field. Consequently, each student will leave the school with at least entry-level job skills and the facility in basic academic subjects to enable him to enter into further education.

In summary, career education

1. provides job information
2. develops job entry skills
3. helps students develop attitudes about the personal, psychological, social, and economic significance of work
4. develops self-awareness in each individual
5. matches student interests and abilities with potential careers
6. guarantees placement into an entry level job or further education for every student

The state of Washington's program is a highly developed, well thought out and valuable one. It is, in fact, exactly what President Nixon had suggested, and may well serve as a prototype. However, it is the product of years of evolution of the concept, and must be regarded in this light. A variety of material has been published by the Coordinating Council, some of which we will be quoting in this and subsequent chapters.

Mr. Louis Bruno, the State Superintendent of Public Instruction, stated in one publication, "This is the time when education must deal with reality. For most of our young people, the world of work is a soon to be realized fact. We have taken the position that the educational process has an integral role in helping the student to achieve self-support in such a manner that self-respect is maintained."

While every school starting out on a program of career education certainly cannot begin with a highly developed program such as Washington's, every school can initiate a good program. If you accept the basic thesis—that career education is a branch of learning we, as educators, cannot continue to neglect, and if you are willing to do something about it, you too can have a fine program. You will find guidelines for it outlined in this book.

Your program will of necessity be different from Washington's—but not necessarily superior or inferior. This is especially true in the elementary and the junior high schools. Washington's program may serve, in some respects, as a model, but you should vary your own program as you and your staff deem necessary to meet the needs of your students and your community.

Any Career Education Program is better than none at all. Any awareness you develop in a child's mind is better than none. Any specific career information you impart is better than none.

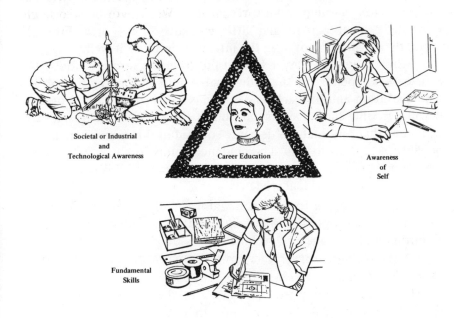

Maryland State Department of Education

EVERY SCHOOL NEEDS A CAREER
EDUCATION PROGRAM

There are many reasons why every school needs Career Education. Every school, big or small—elementary, junior or senior high— but every school—needs it. Every child is entitled to this type of relevant education, this vital information. Let us see why.

1. Look first at the statistic with which we began this chapter: *"2.5 million young people each year graduate from high school, or drop out of high school or college with no planned career, and few, if any, marketable skills."* Some of them live in your community as well as in mine; indeed they are to be found all over the nation. If we question why this is true, we receive some strange answers. It is an interesting experiment to ask your faculty this question: "There are over two million young people in our country without marketable skills. Some are in our community. Why should this be true?"

We have been told, repeatedly, "This is not our problem." Or, "This education should be done in the home. It's the parents' responsibility. It's the parents who should do this educating." But should they? More important—*do they?* We're afraid the answer is a rousing "No." Short of asking "What do you want to be when you grow up?" most parents give little guidance in this area. Furthermore, they really do not have the information to do it well.

What about the Career Education Programs in our schools? Of course this depends on the individual school system, or school—its administration and its teachers. If there is a formal, definite program, it will probably have been taught; but if there is not, the chances are very slim that any material is being covered in this area. There is one possible exception to this. The guidance counselors may be working with some students on career choice—but generally this is with small groups—or with individual students.

Teachers need a formal curriculum to guide them. It is our aim to help you to supply this. You will find the guidelines you will need all outlined here—concepts, techniques, lesson plans.

2. *According to* The New York Times *of December 4, 1972, there are 13 million Americans being supported by public assistance.* While it is undoubtedly true that many of these people are not able to work because of illness or because they are the mothers of young children, there are many who could work—if they had the skills to offer prospective employers. Some localities are attempting to train

those who are physically capable of working—to teach them skills that will lead to employment.

We have the youngsters in our schools for twelve years, more or less. Why haven't we taught all of those who do not plan to continue their education skills which will help them to earn their livings? Those who have elected to go to vocational or technical schools have gotten such training but those who have attended academic high schools have not. The comprehensive high school is one answer to the problem—and is an integral part of any Career Education Program.

3. *Unskilled jobs are disappearing at a phenomenal rate, but unskilled people are not.* Congressman Herman Badillo of New York City, in discussing his experiences as an immigrant who arrived here from Puerto Rico with no skills, has said that in a relatively few years the jobs available to him when he first came here have disappeared. He set pins in a bowling alley, washed dishes, and ran an elevator. All of these jobs have now completely, or almost completely, vanished. They have been phased out by technological advances.

When advertisements for unskilled laborers appear in the newspapers far more people apply than can be hired.

Does it not seem inconceivable that a person can attend school for twelve years, graduate, and not have a single skill—or the definite intention to learn one?

4. *The number of students who are not motivated to do well in school is due, in part, to the failure of educators to make education meaningful.* One of the most graphic examples of this situation is an interview of the young people dropping out of high school in your community. When you question them, you will probably discover that not only are they unskilled, but they also cannot because it was not taught to them, comprehend that every school level should be a preparation for further schooling or for specific jobs. Most often they are negatively conditioned to schooling under any circumstances.

At all educational levels the outcry has been for relevant education. The education offered in both colleges and lower schools has been just as irrelevant in terms of earning a living. When a youngster cannot grasp a subject, often he thinks, "Why should I bother? What good is this, anyway?" He doesn't ask the question aloud, and it goes unanswered.

We usually offer him courses he will never use. Sometimes we hide behind the magic word "background." This canopy can cover a multitude of impractical information. Think about your own education—and think about the curriculum you are offering to your students. How much has really changed since the time you went to school? Yet, look at how many technological improvements have been developed—in just the last decade.

The average or slow students must see the necessity for getting an "education"—but *we* must accept responsibility for giving them one that will improve their lives. Career education will. It will because it is related directly to their future lives. A young man introduced to a machine shop decides, "This is for me. I love working with this equipment." The quiet little girl in the corner suddenly perks up. Her eyes develop a sparkle. She has just realized she could work in a hospital laboratory. "I wanted to be a nurse, but I hate the sight of blood," she told her teacher. "If I work in a bacteriology laboratory, I can help people—without seeing blood." "I know I'm good in arithmetic—but I don't want to be a teacher. I thought that was the only career for someone who liked arithmetic. Then we studied actuarial work, and I really think the person talking about it was talking directly to me," a junior high school student reports. Developing awareness of careers in elementary or junior high schools accomplishes this, and can and should motivate the students.

5. *There is a lack of skilled workers trained to do technical work.* James B. Conant once stated, "Those who, because of population mobility and the reputed desire of employers to train their own employees, would limit vocational education to general rather than specific skills, ought to bear in mind the importance of motivation in any kind of school experience." How many of our children lack motivation because they realize their education is leading them nowhere?

As an example of a state which has developed successful programs in this area, let us consider Massachusetts. Comprehensive vocational-technical schools are being developed there—a "new type of vocational-technical education designed to teach youth to know a craft, not vaguely . . . but with precision and with the ability to change as the craft changes."

This type of career education is made available to students of high school age. In describing its program in MOVE (the word stands for Massachusetts Opportunities in Vocational Education) the Bureau of Vocational Education states, "Publication MOVE is dedicated to the realization that automation, advanced technology and an electronic space age have created a new labor market. Convincing predictions indicate that only 50% of all high school graduates will go on to college, and that 21 million youngsters throughout the nation will not be college graduates in the 1970s. Industrial technological requirements project that a supportive task force of three technicians for every scientist and engineer will be needed. Supply and demand projections for the 1970s estimate that the largest percentage of manpower deficiencies will occur among the graduates of technical schools. This study further indicates a deficit of 34% in the working technician category, while scientific and engineering deficits will be reduced to 14%. In the medical category, the deficit for doctors will be a mere 4%.

To this end, the Commonwealth of Massachusetts has taken the initiative and moved to provide the technical training necessary to satisfy the sophisticated labor requirements for the 1970s."

This is education motivated by the knowledge that a career—a career with a future—is waiting—just as soon as one's schooling is completed.

6. *Students are unaware of the connection between years of education and future income.* For the year 1970, the Bureau of Census published this information. (The salaries given assume the person will work 40 years in his lifetime.)

A person who has less than an elementary school education will earn less than $213,505 in his working lifetime.

A person who has graduated from elementary school will earn less than $276,755.

A person who has from one to three years of a high school education will earn $308,305.

A person who has graduated from high school will earn $371,094.

A person who has from one to three years of college will earn $424,280.

A person who has graduated from college will earn $584,062.

A person who has done one year of postgraduate work, will earn $636,119 or more.

An educational transformation has taken place in the United States according to *The New York Times* (December 7, 1972). As indicated in a population survey report, the typical American now has almost four more years of education than he did as recently as 1940.

The report, like earlier studies, found a strong relationship between schooling and income. "The more years of school completed, the higher one's annual earnings. For instance, among employed men who earned $15,000 or more last year, the median education level was 15.2 years—more than three years of college.

Among those who earned less than $3,000, the education median was 10.7, less than three years of high school.

"The highest education level was for white collar workers earning $15,000 or more—16.3 years, or part of a year of graduate study. The lowest was for farm workers earning less than $3,000—8.7 years or part of a year of high school."

Our young people are not always given this type of information. Many times it comes as a shock to them. Furthermore, they often have very unrealistic ideas in regard to wages and skills.

Where would a young person get this information? He may learn it in school—if he is fortunate enough to have had courses in careers or occupations—but very often he is not so fortunate. His parents do not have the information to give him. Again, this is where the Career Education Program enters the picture. It builds an awareness of the world of work, of the educational requirements for various careers, and of the financial rewards for one's labors. We have summarized this in two words, which we have used literally hundreds of times—"Education pays."

7. *There is a wealth of career education material, but it is often not offered to the children.* Frequently it is buried in the counselors' office, or on the library shelves. For example, consider careers in new industries. Electronic data processing should be introduced. Our young people know the word "computer," but how often have they encountered the various careers existing in the field—from programming to key punch operating?

Opportunities for careers in environmental sciences will grow in the future—but do your students realize this?

Counselors have a great variety of career information to give to their young counselees—but how much time can they possibly devote to giving it? It is hoped that in a full Career Education Program they will be very instrumental in helping the teachers present it to their classes.

Teachers, too, have not related occupations to their subject matter. The science teacher is in an ideal situation to introduce careers in scientific or health fields. The question is, why does he not do so? A Career Education Program puts it into the curriculum—in a meaningful way.

8. *Many young people do not know of the financial aid available to them.* There is a tremendous amount of Federal as well as private aid that goes unused, as well as the vast quantities that are utilized. The problem is that this area, too, has often been kept secret. Grants, scholarships, college employment and, of course,

student loans (guaranteed by the Federal government), are all means by which a young person can support himself, and pay for his education. This knowledge and assistance in applying for the funding have been heretofore handled by the counselors. It is our thesis that it should, rather, be part of the Career Education Program where it will reach many more young people.

Children are missing opportunities and are not going on for additional training because they are uneducated in education-financing. This is particularly true in the large, urban schools. It is another reason your school and every school needs a Career Education Program. Career education places a great value on each individual, and on helping and in some cases training him for his place in the world of work.

9. *The Career Education Program will attempt to reach those young people for whom economic success in not a primary goal.* These students often possess a deep commitment to the service of their fellow men. They will be better able to serve them if they are qualified as skilled artisans, health technicians, social work aides, teachers, or environmental technicians. These are young people who may or may not want to go to college, and who need to be equipped with skills. Most of them will complete their high school educations—and therefore we will have opportunities to educate them. If they are truly idealists, we shall enable them to make real contributions to human welfare.

ESTABLISHING SPECIFIC GOALS FOR YOUR CAREER EDUCATION PROGRAM

Of course the goals you establish for your program will depend, for the most part, on the educational level of your school. An elementary school will obviously have different goals from those of a junior high, and so on. However, if you are initiating a Career Education Program in a high school for young people who have never had such a program before, you will have to help them "catch up." Each of the goals listed is to be taught on the children's level. It is obvious that a trip to a grocery store might be boring for a high school student—unless the manager discusses the business on an adult level. A sixth grader might be introduced to drafting techniques, or a first year high school student made aware of exactly what tasks are performed and which skills are required to become a draftsman. It depends on the teacher and his acceptance of Bruner's concept—that the child be taught at his level of comprehension.

Another factor that would influence your selection of goals would be the aspirational level of your students. Do most of them go on to college—or only a small percentage? Do most of them remain in your community—or move away? What percentage leaves school after graduation to enter the work force? What percentage drops out of high school? All of these questions should be considered as you select appropriate objectives.

Still another consideration would be the amount of time and funding you can devote to your Career Education Program. The program of the state of Washington is far more involved than that of other areas of the country, as has already been pointed out. But, even if you can only give one course to one grade once a week, that is preferable to none at all.

The following list of objectives is a basis from which you may work, but is hardly all-inclusive. You may find many others you wish to include as you work with your staff on the selection of goals.

MAJOR GOALS OR OBJECTIVES OF
A CAREER EDUCATION PROGRAM

1. *To help each youngster develop an awareness of himself and of his place in the world of work.*

The student brings with him both attitudes and knowledge about himself. As he matures, he realizes he has certain talents and he develops ideas in regard to his possible place in the world of work.

Through career education, his home, and his community experiences, the student will be introduced to the many careers from which he may choose. He will be encouraged to learn as much as he can about himself so that he will make his career choice based on self-knowledge.

This involves guidance and counseling as well as instruction. All three, however, are aimed to help the young person develop self-awareness and self-direction; to expand his occupational awareness and aspirations; and to develop appropriate attitudes about the personal and social significance of work.

2. *To develop an awareness of the huge variety of careers possible.*

The *Dictionary of Occupational Titles,* published by the U.S. Department of Labor, lists over 25,000 job titles. While many overlap, there are thousands and thousands of careers from which a young person may choose. One of our major tasks is to make him aware of many of them. It is surprising how many he has never encountered before.

The *Occupational Outlook Handbook,* also published by the Labor Department, has divided the various careers into fifteen career clusters, and we will use this classification as our basis in developing a curriculum.

3. *To develop an awareness of what specific tasks each career actually entails.*

It is always surprising to discover that children often don't know what it is, exactly, that *their fathers or mothers* actually do. Oh, they may know, "My father is an accountant," but when asked, "What does an accountant do?" they are at a loss. One child answered wisely, "He takes care of accounts," but when asked what accounts were, she shrugged her shoulders and looked embarrassed.

When a student evidences an interest in a career, even a slight interest, one of his first tasks should be to learn the specific duties it involves. Consider the young people who think they would like to "return to the land," and become farmers. Once they learn they have to milk the cows at 5:00 A.M., their goals may change.

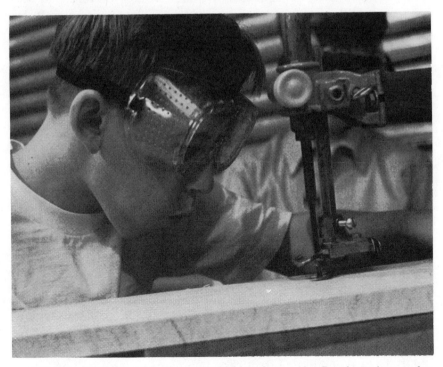

Washington State Council for Occupational Education   Alex Crewdson, photographer

4. *To develop an awareness of the career ladder concept and of the various levels of careers, depending on the education or training required.*

A career ladder is a series of jobs within the same major industry, ranging from semiskilled, lower paying jobs to highly skilled, higher paying careers. The interesting point to note is that a person may choose where he wishes to place himself on the ladder—and prepare accordingly. He may place himself on the ladder in a variety of ways; one is by entering at the bottom, and working his way up through a series of jobs. Another is by taking courses that will train him, and then entering the field on a higher level. There are career levels in many industries that offer these routes of advancement.

The unskilled laborer is employed to do some type of physical work. He is often, but not always, required to be able to read and to write. Semiskilled workers are people who usually learn the skills they require on their jobs. When they operate relatively uncomplicated machines, they are called operators. The next category, in terms of a knowledge of skills, is the skilled worker or craftsman who has many skills, usually related and which are then called a craft. He has learned them in one of a number of ways—through many years of experience on-the-job, through an apprenticeship, or through vocational schooling. Technically trained people are in the next educational level, and are usually the graduates of technical institutes or two-year colleges. The top level, educationally speaking, is the professional or managerial level. The professionals in most careers except sports or entertainment have graduated from four-year colleges, or have even done postgraduate work. In the case of people in managerial positions, they are often college graduates with business experience.

5. *To make every academic subject area more meaningful and relevant through the use of the basic concepts of career education.*

Students have often complained of the lack of practicality in their educations. When we teach language arts, mathematics, sciences, or social studies in terms of abstracts (the so-called pure approach) their value is diminished in the eyes of many young people. This is particularly true of those boys and girls who are not academically inclined, and whose strengths lie in other areas. We sometimes neglect to give them the most basic of tools, such as the ability to read and write effectively.

By using a career development theme, we are able to emphasize the practicality of what we are teaching—and use this for motivation.

By giving the students actual work experiences, we are able to show the nonacademically inclined student that he, too, is able to be productive.

6. *To develop an awareness of the connection between academic achievement in the elementary school, its continuation in high school, and its further continuation in college.*

There are in most schools a number of students who achieve well in the lower grades, and then in high school. When they continue in college, they usually do reasonably well or very well there. Educators often do not realize the need for them to get a foundation in the lower schools that will prepare them for college or for the world of work. The relationship of work habits, past, present and future with academic success is very marked, *yet they do not see it.*

A student who shows he is not academically inclined, but is motivated to go to college, needs additional education and guidance. He may still choose to go to college after high school, but he should do this knowing he will need remedial help in addition to having to do his college work. Since he has shown he is not achieving well academically, he should be given information in regard to the other avenues of education available to him—the vocational or technical courses he may take, and the careers that will then open to him.

The percentage of students entering colleges today is 50 percent of the population. The percentage that finally graduates is 12 percent. Whan happens to the other 38 percent?

Individuals have many talents, other than academic ones, to utilize. However, it is far more difficult for a child who has done poorly academically to succeed in college than it is for one who has done reasonably well. It is certainly not impossible. But, of late, educators and the public have been giving young people the impression they can go from non-achieving in the elementary or high school to achieving in college. It isn't that easy! A child who does not achieve all through elementary or high school has a far less chance for success than one who has achieved. Isn't he entitled to know this?

7. *To make education meaningful to all of the students—those planning to terminate their education immediately after high school, or who plan to attend college, technical, or vocational school afterward.*

This requires a review of the entire curriculum your students are being given in terms of its value to them in their situation. This does not imply that children should not be introduced to literature or to fine music. There is most assuredly a place in the school's curriculum for enrichment of all kinds. But they should certainly be taught how to write a business letter, how to apply for a job, and how to fill out applications for everything from Social Security cards to college applications.

The growth of the comprehensive high school, which offers career preparatory courses, takes this factor into consideration. We have trained students in business subjects for years, and also in various vocational fields. Now the comprehensive high school is entering the technical fields and preparing young people to go directly into some of them—such as medical technology.

Until recently, the youngster who chose to go to vocational high school or to take business subjects in the academic high school was prepared to earn a living. The young person who took the general course was not prepared for any career and all too frequently his education ended when he dropped out of school or when he graduated with a general diploma—and no skills.

8. *To understand the economic facts of life and their connection with education or training.*

The statistics concerning correlation of education and income should be covered in many classes in the same way we cover such subject areas as American history. It is essential that we make sure each student grasps their significance. Most young people are totally unaware of the connection between education and income and, as a result, never develop to their full potential.

While the statistics do change, the fact is that the relationship between education in terms of skills and income remains the same.

Unlike countries in Europe, for example, we have enjoyed a great degree of social mobility—as a direct result of the ability of a person to "work his way up in the world." One of the best ways he can do this is through education.

9. *To develop an awareness of the need for the young woman as well as the young man to learn skills and to prepare for a future career.*

Today women make up 40 percent of the labor force. Housekeeping is no longer the arduous, demanding task it once was, and many married women, when their children have grown up or when they wish to supplement the family income, seek employment. This is an eventuality to be prepared for. Another is the possibility of the young woman having the need to earn a living because she never marries, or is divorced or widowed. For whatever reason, all young women should think in terms of career preparation.

This preparation may take place in high school or in college. However, just as young men need specific skills, so do young women. Furthermore, many areas are opening up for women which have never been open to them before. It is essential that they be made aware of this.

10. *To develop an awareness of the time and money required for a person to be trained or educated for a specific career.*

It is almost shocking to learn that young people have very little idea of how to prepare for a specific career. They must learn which schools and colleges offer preparation for some careers, which institutes and vocational schools prepare them for others, and which they can be trained for in their high schools. They need to learn, too, what the length of the course is, and what the tuition and other expenses involved are. Here, too, a lack of specific education is often evident. There are many tuition-free colleges, both four and two year, throughout the United States offering excellent education and training with a minimum of expense to the student.

11. *To develop an awareness of the availability of funds to every student for furthering his education.*

There are many scholarships which are not awarded each year because there is a lack of applicants for them. The same is true of grants. Your children should be prepared to apply for them. Very often they are not and many who could receive stipends which would make it possible to devote themselves wholeheartedly to their education are forced to take jobs to support themselves.

Other funding is available through special jobs which are created by the colleges. Furthermore, students may always get student loans—on which they pay no interest until after they graduate.

Vital as this information is, it is amazing how many young people are unaware of it.

12. *To develop the concept of career by choice, not chance, and to develop techniques for doing full career studies.*

There are in the United States a very large number of people working in careers for which they did not prepare, or did not choose. Even when one selects his career, there is a chance he will be unhappy in it. When he glides into it, without planning and without consideration, the chances of unhappiness are far, far greater. By making your student aware of the great variety of career offerings, and by helping him to take into consideration his talents his abilities and his interests, you can have a tremendous effect on his future happiness.

Full career studies include in-depth analysis of what is involved in the day-to-day performance of a particular career, what the educational training for it is, what salary it pays, what the employment prospects are, and what type of person will be successful in the career being studied. The student is given the tools to do this type of analysis on any career in which he is interested, so that he can do so at any point in his life if he wishes to make a career change.

13. *To develop methods for the young people to examine their personalities and attempt to find careers that will bring them job satisfaction.*

Personality is a term used to describe the manner in which a person behaves and the particular way in which he reacts to a variety of situations. He can learn to project these into the possible job situation. It takes into consideration, too, the manner in which he reacts to other people, because this can seriously affect his functioning in a career. Therefore, it is necessary to keep this in mind when one seeks to find a career that he will enjoy and which will bring him pleasure and feelings of accomplishment.

14. *To offer specific vocational or technical training to those who plan to terminate their education after high school.*

It is essential that this type of education be geared to the specific needs of the businesses in the community. Just as we train our young people in stenography or bookkeeping, so we should train them in technical skills as well. Technical education, for example, is offered in Massachusetts in both the high school and the posthigh school levels. The same is true of New York City, in special high schools. However, it is essential that every school offer every pupil some vocational or technical alternative—so that no one graduates from high school, as one-third of our students have, with a general diploma that indicates he does not possess any skills which would make him employable.

15. *To offer academic preparation, including advance placement courses, to those preparing to enter college.*

At the same time, these young people should be given vocational or technical training so that, should they drop out of college, as about 38 of the 50 percent of our population that enters does, they have skills to turn to, which would make them employable.

The last five months of school for many high school seniors are often a waste of time. They could, in the last year, learn some skills—if our programs are geared toward this—as they should be. Advanced placement takes care of this in some cases, but not in all. Since the number of pupils who leave college is so great, they should be protected by what we offer to them in high school. This is, of course, the *raison d'etre* for the comprehensive high school. When it functions well, it can do an excellent job of career preparation for everyone.

The academic preparation includes training for choosing a college, for calculations of costs, for selection of courses, and for entering into extracurricular college activities. It takes into consideration study habits and doing research and term papers.

16. *To develop an awareness of the availability of training and education at any time in the individual's life—enabling him to obtain new skills, and therefore to make himself more valuable to his employer.*

Too many adults feel frozen in their jobs and do not realize the mobility our society offers them. It is our task, as educators, to show our students these educational options. A person may, for instance, decide to take a job upon graduation from high school. Then, a year later, he or she returns to a posthigh school institution for further training. Perhaps he or she will not return for five or ten years. However, an awareness of this course of action is essential.

The same option of "return for more education" should be offered to the high school dropout who, in later years, wishes to return for further formal schooling.

Summary

An ideal Career Education Program provides job information; develops job entry skills; helps students develop attitudes about the personal, psychological, social, and economic significance of work; develops self-awareness in each individual; matches student interests and abilities with potential careers; and guarantees placement into an entry level job or further education for every student.

In instituting your program, you may not be in a position to accomplish all of the objectives that follow, but any you can achieve are worthwhile. These include: developing an awareness in every student of the world of work, and familiarizing each one with the huge number and variety of careers available to him. Every young man or woman should become familiar with the tasks that make up a career on a day-to-day basis. He or she should be given an awarness of the career ladder concept, and of the fact that one is able to work one's way up in a given area. The student should encounter the various levels of careers, and realize these are dependent on the training or education the individual has received. He should be *helped to see the connection between his work in elementary, junior, and senior high school, and the prognosis for his success in college. By establishing courses that will help him in his future life, we are able to make education meaningful for every child. The economic facts of life should be presented to the young people, along with their relationship to skills and training.*

Young women should be shown the need for them to plan their careers. Time and money are required if a young person is to obtain a college education, and he should be made aware of the requirements. He should also be taught where he can receive assistance in the funding of his education. The concept of career by choice, not chance, should be presented, as well as the effect one's personality should have on this choice. By offering specific vocational and technical training to young people still in high school, we can prevent a high school graduate from being unskilled when he seeks employment. We must offer academic preparation for college, as well. We should also give our students an awareness of the role they are to play as workers in our society. They should understand, too, the assistance which they may get from the educational and vocational counselor. Since some of our students will ultimately go into business for themselves, there should be some education in this area. As we establish our Career Education Program, we should attempt to involve parents, community members, faculty and the students so that the program becomes a vital part of the curriculum from kindergarten through the twelfth grade.

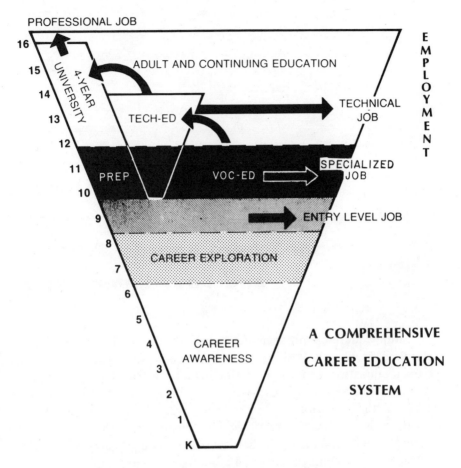

Center for Career Development, Mesa, Arizona

2

How to Gain Acceptance for a Career Education Program from School Boards, Parents and Your Community

Sidney Marland, in speaking before the Council of Chief State School Officers, put it directly to us, as educators, when he said, "Career education cannot be defined solely in Washington. Revolution doesn't happen because government suggests it. We can ask many of the questions, we can help with funds, but if career education is to be the revolutionary instrument that the times demand, it will be defined in hard and urgent debate across the land by teachers, laymen, students and administrators in months to come. Let that debate start now.

"The Chief State School Officers, without a single exception, agreed to commit themselves to the educational revolution that is now taking form.

"The future of that revolution will depend on the support it receives from the people of America—especially from its educators."[1]

Certainly it is the administrators who will be instrumental in making the decisions concerning the directions education will take in the years ahead. We have been, for the past fifteen years, suffering from the "Sputnik syndrome." We have pushed and prodded our children, trying to make all of them college material. As a result, while 50 percent of our high school graduates do enter college, 38 percent of them drop out. We are teaching 80 percent of our young

---

[1]Career Education #5 Dept. HEW, DHEW Public. #(OE 73-00501)

people what only 20 percent of them need. The others are getting little of practical value from their educations.

It is with this in mind that we urge administrators to make curricular changes that will prepare young people for the world of work—as well as for attending college. These changes have been grouped into a program called Career Education.

What is the role of the superintendent of schools, and of the principals and other administrators in regard to career education?

First it is to become completely aware of the value of career education. If you are convinced of its value, and become enthused and involved with it, we believe you will be able to become an effective sales person for it in your community. Few concepts introduced into the policy circles of American education have ever been met with such instant acclaim. It has emerged at a moment when there is a great deal of dissatisfaction with what we, as a profession, have been able to accomplish with our young people. (Thirty percent drop out before graduating from high school.) It promises to attack and improve some of the apparent sources of that dissatisfaction. (Why aren't 15,000 school hours, representing the time a child spends with us from kindergarten through 12th grade sufficient to give that child some specific skills so that he is equipped to do a *specific* job, when it is time for him to go to work?)

We, as educators and administrators, are the ones who have to carry the ball. We are the ones who are being taken to task and told to make radical improvements. Here is a program that can have a truly lasting effect on every youngster passing through our schools. It is up to us to bring this program to the attention of our local school boards and to our state departments of education as well. We are in a perfect position to do so. We know our children—and our community—and we know our teachers. (If we don't, it is really a sad state of affairs.)

As was stated before, career education is a series of concepts rather than a specific plan. A school or a school system need not adopt every aspect; in fact, a full Career Education Program for every grade from kindergarten through twelfth is a very long-range objective. There are other objectives, however, that may be established and worked toward almost immediately.

There are many experimental programs going on today that you will read about in these pages. For example, in the state of Washington career education has been in focus since 1967. When elementary school principal Richard Erskine describes his curriculum he calls it a "coordinated effort for occupationally oriented education from K through 6" and he will tell you that "It's risky when you do something different." According to a booklet produced by the Washington State Coordinating Council for Occupational Education, "Erskine has turned his school into an occupational awareness camp." "Every teacher, every student is involved," he says and also claims one of the highest ratios of parent involvement anywhere. They volunteer to teach subjects such as typing, carpentry, and electricity. "This is not just to let the students fool around with equipment," he explains, "but to teach the skills and study about the jobs that go with those skills."

Unruffled by the notion he might be taking a risk in using noncertified parents, he states simply that "It's always risky when you do something different. It's more important to have the help." He says teachers are encouraged to take on projects to get the kids into the community and out of the classroom.[2]

SPECIAL MATERIAL IS FORTHCOMING
FROM THE OFFICE OF EDUCATION

The U.S. Office of Education is sponsoring a large number of educational projects, among which one of the largest is the Comprehensive Career Education Model (called, usually, CCEM). Six school districts across the country have been chosen to work together in the designing and testing of a curriculum model for career development education which will then be distributed nationally. (The six districts are Atlanta, Ga.; Hackensack, N.J.; Jefferson County, Colo.; Los Angeles, Calif.; Mesa, Arizona; Pontiac, Mich.) The project is being administered by a staff of career education specialists at Ohio State University.

The CCEM approaches career education as a long-term, developmental process involving personal growth as well as the acquirement of skills.

In Hackensack, teachers have been assigned the preparation of units covering all grade levels except kindergarten, and related to various academic areas. The units are actually written by the teachers in the district. These units will be used as part of the existing curriculum and do not form a separate or additional one. They will be presented as part of relevant academic areas.

Each of the units is intended either to help students learn about a specific career field (one of the fifteen "clusters") or to help them

---

[2]Washington State Coordinating Council for Occupational Education. What about Vocational Ed. Part 2.

develop a set of understandings or competencies needed to achieve a career goal. For example, unit for grades 7-9 has been developed dealing with careers in government which will be presented through social studies classes. The unit utilizes a number of approaches including field experiences, simulations, role-playing exercises, media presentations, and research assignments to help students explore the wide variety of careers in government service. At the elementary level, a grade 1 unit in water purification teaches basic science and numbers and skills through actual experiments in testing and purifying polluted water.[3]

In addition to the curriculum you will find in the second part of this book you will be able to obtain material such as this, and a great deal more, from the Office of Education.

One of the advantages of introducing a new program is the *esprit de corps* you can engender with it. As we outline the steps we suggest you take, we do so with the idea of motivating both the students and the teachers. (There is always the possibility that you may apply for Federal funding for an experimental project and this, too, can add to the excitement.) Any experimental situation, when fully explained, creates its own excitement—excitement of a positive nature. Furthermore, because of the entire basis of this program, the students should be enthused about it—provided it is presented to them effectively. This presentation should be one of the high points of the school year. It will be discussed subsequently.

HOW TO PREPARE FOR, AND INTRODUCE THE CAREER EDUCATION PROGRAM TO THE LOCAL SCHOOL BOARD, THE PARENTS, AND THE COMMUNITY

No program can ever succeed if there is no reason for its being. Career education is no exception. Your first task, then, is to show specifically how your school would benefit from such a program.

Establishing a Committee

One of the first steps you should take is to establish a committee. The purpose and function of this group is to work out a rationale for the presentation of the Career Education Program, and a tentative program showing the changes to be made in the curriculum of your school to incorporate career education. Your committee

---

[3]*Hackensack Public Schools,* Vol. I, Number III, September, 1972, Hackensack, N. J.

should include yourself, one or two other administrators, your guidance counselors, teachers and, if you so desire, students and parents.

In planning for career education, your counselors should be considered key people. They have received training in the presentation of occupational information, and may have been involved in counseling young people in career choice and career planning. (This would depend, of course, on the age level of your students.) They are familiar with the sources of occupational resource material. Counseling must be an integral part of your Career Education Program. You may count on your counselors to:

1. Assist in the development of the rationale for your Career Education Program. (This includes compiling statistics to show why your students would benefit from such a program.)

2. Assist the teachers in the development of the curriculum.

3. Conduct workshops for your teachers in regard to the presentation of the curriculum.

4. Order supplies and materials.

5. Counsel individual youngsters or groups of students.

6. Train paraprofessionals and aides.

7. Possibly coordinate the entire program. (You may prefer to have an administrator do this.)

The teachers will, of course, be important members of this committee and ultimately determine the success of the program. As a rule of thumb, if you are working in an elementary school, one teacher per grade is generally adequate. In a junior or senior high school, one per four-classes seems to offer adequate representation. Invite every teacher to participate. However, it is vital that you seek out those teachers who are enthusiastic individuals, who will become involved in the program, and who will make contributions to it. If your committee is composed of remote individuals who offer little in the way of suggestions, one or two persons will end up doing all of the work. This is to be avoided if at all possible.

You may choose to have students and parents represented as well. The Student Government and the Parent Teacher Associations represent these groups, and may be invited to send representatives if you so desire. You know your school and the manner in which it functions. We believe it is a good idea to include these groups in the planning stages because you will need parental approval, and the purpose of the program is to have a favorable motivational effect on your students.

Doing Follow-Up Studies of
Your Graduates and Former Students

As was stated, no program can ever succeed if there is no reason for its being. To show why your students would benefit from Career Education, you will do well to use a number of statistics. Some of them involve follow-up studies of your graduates and of the pupils who left high school without graduating.

Once you have your committee established, one of the most effective ways to obtain vital statistics is by doing follow-up studies. The following forms may be sent out to your graduates or former students. If your school is too new to have a sizable number, you may have to change the format of the request—but it would still be worthwhile to survey your community.

The first form is one which would be suitable to use if yours is a high school.

Your School Heading

Dear _____

As a former student of this school, you are in a position to be of assistance to us in a matter we consider to be vitally important. Would you be kind enough to return this form to us as soon as you possibly can. We are considering many important changes in our curriculum and the information you give us will, in large measure, dictate those changes. We appreciate your help.

Sincerely,

Principal

1. In which year did you leave this school? _____

2. Did you graduate_____, transfer_____, or leave_____? (If the third choice, please explain. _____

_____

_____

3. What are you doing today? _____

    a. Are you working full time_____

    b. Are you working part time_____

    c. Are you going to school full time_____

    d. Are you going to school part time_____

4. If your answer is "Yes" to either item (c) or (d), where are you attending school? _____

5. Did you get a job immediately after leaving school or graduating? _____

6. Did any course you took in this school equip you for a specific job? _____

7. Did you go on for further education? _____

    a. Did you go to a vocational or technical school? _____

    b. Did you go to a two-year college? _____

    c. Did you go to a four-year college? _____

8. If your answer was "yes" to 7,

    a. What course did you take? _____

    b. What was your goal? _____

9. Did you reach your goal? _____

10. Did you receive any occupational or career information while you attended this school? _____

11. Did you receive adequate guidance services while you were a student here? _____

12. If you have any suggestions as to how we can improve our program in terms of career education, please jot them down here.

_____

_____

_____

_____

_____

Please use the other side of this sheet if you require more space.

Our sincere thanks for your help.

The next form is one for you to use if yours is an elementary, intermediate or junior high school.

Use the same first paragraph as in the previous form. However, use the following questions:

1. In which year did you graduate from this school? _____

2. Which high school did you attend? _____

3. Which course did you take in high school? _____

4. At the time you chose your high school course, did you have a specific objective? _____

5. If your answer above was "yes," what was it? _____

6. Did you reach that objective? _____

7. Did you get a job immediately after high school? _____

8. Did you go on for additional education after high school? _____

9. If your answer to 8 was "yes," which school did you attend? _____

_____

10. Which course did you take? _____

11. Did you complete it? _____

12. What are you doing today? _____

13. Did you receive any occupational or career information while you were a student in this school? _____

14. If you have any suggestions in regard to how we can improve our program in terms of career education, please jot them down here.

_____

_____

_____

If you require more space, please use the reverse side of this form, or add additional sheets of paper. Our very sincere thanks for your response.

Very truly yours,

Principal

If your school has been in existence for a number of years, you may decide exactly how many of your graduates you would like to survey. You may do this in one of several ways:

a. Survey the entire class of one, five and ten years ago.
b. Spot check, by sending questionnaires to 10 to 20% of each graduating class.

In either event, use your responses to determine:

1. The number of your graduates who graduated from high school and went into the labor market.
2. The number who had courses in high school that prepared them for jobs.
3. The number who went on for further education in vocational schools.
4. The number who went on to two-year colleges and dropped out.
5. The number who went on to two-year colleges and completed their courses.
6. The number who went on to four-year colleges and dropped out.
7. The number who went on to four-year colleges and graduated.

These statistics, more than anything else, can show you the goals your Career Education Program should assume. What were the needs of your students?

There are other factors to consider, too. Has the group changed drastically for any reason? Is it different now, socio-economically, from what it was when these students graduated? If not, then your statistics should hold true as projections.

You may also use the information available at the local office of the United States Employment Office. Discuss your projected program with them, asking in which areas most of the population finds employment and for which skills training would be the most valuable in terms of job opportunities.

A check of the help-wanted columns in both the local newspapers and the papers of the largest city in your state will also reveal those career areas which are in demand.

If there are any large employers in your locality, a representative of yours may interview their personnel managers to determine where there are jobs to be had.

The results of the various surveys we have listed will be vital to the planning of your actual program. Before this can be done, however, you should know exactly how much has been taught in your classes in the field of career education.

Determining the State of Your Present Career Education Program

To do this, we suggest you use the following questionnaires:

To Administrators and Counselors:

Name _____

Area of supervision _____

Counselor _____

The following is a survey to help us to prepare for our Career Education Program. In regard to what we have done previously in this area: (The first seven questions are for all schools—elementary, intermediate, junior and senior high.)

1. Are we offering any specific courses in the study of occupations?
2. Have we discussed, by departments, interjecting career information into each subject area? In which career areas has this been done?
3. To how many of our pupils have we been able to offer guidance services in the area of careers?
4. What is the pupil-counselor ratio?
5. Have we developed a resource center that may be used for research in career education?

6. If not, have we adequate materials in the library for such resource? How many reference books? Magazines? Books? Pamphlets? Filmstrips? Films?

7. Have we worked with the teachers on the techniques to be used for career education? How? (Be specific.)

(The next questions are for high schools)

8. Have we specific courses that offer the skills for entry-level jobs? List these courses.

FOR THE FOLLOWING QUESTIONS PLEASE SEPARATE THE RESPONSES FOR MEN AND WOMEN

9. How many of our graduates receive general diplomas?

10. Of those listed in Item 9, how many have taken any courses which would give them marketable skills—such as typing, office machines, and bookkeeping?

11. Have we done any follow-up studies to see where they have gone from here? What were the results?

12. How many of our students have dropped out of school?

13. Have we done any follow-up studies to see where these young people have gone from here?

14. Have we asked for advice from any of our graduates or dropouts in order to improve our guidance program? If so, what were their comments?

A further survey of your program should be made by submitting the following questionnaire to your faculty:

To: All Teachers

Re: Career Education

Teacher's name _____

Subject or subjects taught _____

Grade level _____

We are making a survey of our curriculum in terms of career education. Can you give us a brief statement in regard to the following topics?

1. Have you included any occupational or career information in your teaching? Yes _____ No _____

If your answer is yes, in which units? In what ways?
(Leave adequate space for answers. You may wish to add a phrase to the effect that additional pages may be added to this sheet if necessary.)

2. We are, as you know, interested in developing a Career Education Program in our school. Have you any ideas in regard to the manner in which we can do this? Your suggestions would be very much appreciated.

3. Have you worked with any individual students on career choice? If so, which ones, and in what specific manner? What was the result?

4. Have you taken any courses in any way related to career education?

5. Are you familiar with any materials that would be useful in this area? If so, please list them. Should you have a bibliography in your posession, we would be pleased to have it, for reference use.

6. Have you developed any techniques that you feel would be valuable for use in this area?

7. If we were to establish a Career Education Program, what special aspects of it would you want to see covered in workshops and in-service courses?

These surveys will take from several months to a term to prepare, but they should be, as you can see, the very foundation of any program of career education you would develop. The counselors would generally do most of the correlating and reporting. They will, however, need adequate secretarial help, and it is important that this be supplied to them.

Developing a Tentative Program

After the surveys have been completed, the next step would be the development of a tentative program for your school. This should consist of four aspects:

A. The reasons your specific school and community need a Career Education Program. (These may be taken basically from the list to be found in the first section of Chapter I, which you have modified to fit your needs. Certainly, the national picture is worth including in any listing of reasons, followed by your specific situation.)

B. The goals you wish to establish for your program. (These may be adopted from the listing in the second section of Chapter I. The same reasoning applies here. Consider broad as well as specific objectives.)

Couch your tentative program in language that is easily understood. This is not the time to hide behind jargon or pedagese, because this type of education should be gut-level—and it should be presented as such.

C. The costs involved will depend, of course, on the age level of your students. They may be infinitely less in the elementary and intermediate schools, more in the junior high and, of course, considerably more in high schools. However, the program can be initiated, literally, on a shoe string. *It is the adoption of the philosophy which is important.* Once that has been accepted, it is our firm belief your teachers will be able to develop it, and your community will support it.

In the elementary school, units may be added to your existing curriculum in almost every subject area. You may wish to offer a separate course in occupations in which each child is introduced to the fifteen career clusters.

In the intermediate and junior high schools, specialization in three of these fifteen career clusters is recommended. Here, too, you may wish to offer separate courses in occupations—emphasizing these career clusters, or work them into the regular curriculum.

By the time the young person reaches the high school, it is assumed he will still have time to explore the career clusters, but he will be involved more deeply in one. In his tenth year, he should be offered skill area courses in the career cluster of his choice. It is for this that comprehensive high schools have been established. However, very, very few offer such courses for every one of the fifteen career clusters. Most do have business subjects, and have had them for years. The new health career programs are to be found in some high schools, technical courses in still others. Depending on the needs of your particular community, your high school should develop courses that will prepare your youngsters for earning a living there. At the same time, college preparatory courses are given to all students who plan to attend either two- or four-year colleges.

As you can see, the Career Education Program can start slowly and pick up momentum as it goes along.

D. The actual work to be done in the classroom. In the second section of this book, you will find a complete curriculum, grade by grade, for your Career Education Program. However, unless it is essential that you develop your own plan fully, at this point we suggest that you use sample items without being too specific. The reasons are three fold:

1. It is necessary that the curriculum you use be selected carefully and painstakingly. It can not be done superficially and quickly because you need a program to present.

2. The teachers should be the ones to select and plan activities, based on the objectives that have been established. There will be material from which they can choose, but the lessons must reflect the philosophy of education of your particular school.

3. The program needs continuity. With teachers planning together, they can work up a curriculum that will really be of value to all of the children. For example, they can avoid the duplication that blights much of our education system. They can include techniques that will highly motivate the children at the same time they are teaching them.

Presenting Your Tentative Career Education Program

This is a program we believe will meet with far greater public acceptance than many which have been adopted to date. It is necessary, though, for it to be presented in a manner in which it will be fully understood. For this reason, we feel that if this is done personally, by your committee and yourself, and by people really committed to it, the results must, of necessity, be good.

1. Your program as just outlined would be presented first, of course, to your local school board—as clearly, concisely, and persuasively as possible. Using your statistics and showing the need for the program should be your first step. You may use an overhead projector to present these.

If you need support for increased funds, for additional personnel such as guidance counselors, for example, relate the need directly to the services *every child* will be getting. (This is opposed to the "crisis counseling" often done by counselors in "one-counselor" schools.)

You may wish to invite speakers from the personnel departments of industries found in your area. You might also contact the local representative of the United States Employment Office. You can present facts and figures from the help-wanted columns of your local newspapers.

If there is a Career Education Pilot Project in your area, you may decide to invite a representative to discuss it with your school board, or you may send members of your committee to visit various schools and present their findings.

Prepare a fact sheet and distribute it to every one present.

It is worthwhile to ask members of your committee to present the topics on which they have been working, rather than presenting all of the material yourself.

Of course, you will present your budgetary requests as well.

2. Establish a series of Introductory Career Education Meetings for parents and members of the community.

Again, use the statistics, but present them so that they are readily understood by everyone present. Explain your goals for the program as fully as possible, and include the personnel, the materials, and the other expenditures.

Discuss the need for the participation of members of the community in this program and the fact that parents will be more involved in this than ever before, coming in as speakers and as teachers and inviting the groups to visit them at their places of employment.

Present a fact sheet so that people may discuss the program afterward, with accurate figures available to them.

You may invite any of the speakers listed above to speak at these types of meetings. Any would be very much worthwhile.

3. Hold smaller meetings of the same type. Most of the time there is a better exchange of ideas with a limited number of people. You might wish to do this with members of your Parents Association executive board, or with members of the local Kiwanis or Rotary, whose support would be very worthwhile because of their positions in the business community.

4. Send out a Principal's Newsletter to reach those parents who do not come to meetings. There are a variety of reasons why they do not come, but the fact is often the very parents who should come never appear. By mailing the Newsletter, you will reach many of them. You can use the same fact sheet you distributed at the introductory meetings.

5. Local newspaper coverage of your career education meetings and stories about the program you hope to offer can help engender public suport. It is important that these be very accurate and carefully written, with full explanation of the program. Again, forgive this reminder, but *your enthusiasm and conviction will carry this program along.* When combined with the facts that show the need for it, you cannot lose.

How to Gain Acceptance from Your Teachers and Motivate Them

In presenting and motivating any program, if people are involved in it from the very beginning of the planning stages, they are far more likely to work hard to make it succeed. This is as true of teachers as it is of everyone. Therefore, it is important that you have as many teachers as wish to serve on your tentative and permanent planning committees.

When you reach the stage at which the program has been accepted, a permanent planning committee should be established. This committee may be composed of the same members as the temporary committee, but with as many teachers as possible.

Their task is to develop a curriculum for the entire program, as it will be utilized in your school. In Part Two you will find a curriculum that may be the basis for this. It should be modified, as we have said, to fit your needs, and use the objectives stated in your tentative program. There is a bibliography as well, which will serve as a source of resource material.

No project as extensive as this can be done during school hours. It is necessary that time be allotted for this purpose. You may prefer to designate several weeks during the summer vacation, for which the teachers should be paid. In any event, this work cannot be considered part of a teacher's normal duties. Since career education involves every grade level, it is recommended that provisions be made for each teacher to participate.

As the curriculum is being developed, the counselors should work with the teachers in regard to the special techniques which should be part of the Career Education Program. These will be discussed at length in the second section of the book. After the program is put into operation, a running series of career education workshops for teachers should be established for evaluation and improvement purposes. These should be by grade level, held once a month on school time. In the elementary school this might be done by showing a film in the assembly, on a grade level, while the teachers met. It might be done while the classes were doing research in the library or media center if this is not too taxing on the facilities. It might be arranged while the classes are having physical education, or any subject for which they have another teacher. In the intermediate, junior, or senior high school, this should not be as great a problem, programmingwise. But the meetings are essential—for the sharing of information, and for the establishment of procedures that may be used by groups from all classes on the grade level. For example, on one grade level, the class may be working on transportation. In each class there may be some children interested in truck-driving, particularly over-the-road driving. They may be grouped together, and taken on a trip to an organization that has many such trucks on the road. It is not necessary to take the entire grade—only those children who are especially interested.

At the career education workshops, new techniques may be introduced and discussed. Experiences with films or film strips may be commented upon. The sharing of information is a very basic tool of the Career Education Program. If a particular technique falls flat, it is important to determine the reason why, and to change it. In rare cases, it might be necessary to eliminate it altogether. Workshops give teachers confidence. They serve to alleviate the anxiety that any new program initiates.

Teachers should be encouraged to see this program and the units of work they will be doing as different from other aspects of the regular curriculum. Career education material should be highly personalized. Furthermore, there are no right and wrong answers. The child will respond in terms of his own likes and dislikes. It is the purpose of the program to give him many experiences and many new career areas to think about, but he does not have to make any choices at all until he has been introduced to a large number of them. The trips children take, the speakers they hear, the people they interview—all of these will make the career education units something they will enjoy and look forward to. And if they are shown why career choice is so important, this, in itself, will motivate many of them.

Alleviating Teacher Anxiety

Sources of possible anxiety should be lessened. The fact that there is a curriculum to follow and that workshops will be held to share information should alleviate several. Resource materials will be made available. Part of the development of this program rests on an adequate source of materials. This will be covered in Chapter 5. Furthermore, the teacher will need assistance in her classroom and for this purpose aids, paraprofessionals, college students, and even students within the class may be utilized. This, too, will later be discussed in full.

Another possible way to decrease anxiety is by the establishment of demonstration lessons. These are especially important when the teacher is asked to utilize a technique with which he or she is unfamiliar. Seeing it done in actuality (or on video-tape) can do a great deal to make it less frightening. For example, demonstration lessons have been used to help elementary school teachers get over their reluctance, based on feelings of insecurity, to teach science. They were particularly resistant to having the children do experiments; yet when they saw this type of lesson, discussed it fully, and learned the techniques involved, they became enthusiastic.

Career education lends itself to team teaching. The presentation of some occupational information can easily be done with large groups, which then break up into small groups for discussion purposes. By using this technique, counselors or speakers can address an entire grade level (in an elementary school) without having to give the same speech again and again.

The most important ingredient in any program is the attitudes of the proponents. If they believe in it, are truly involved and anxious to make it interesting, the chances are great that it will succeed. There is one problem, however, and it exists in many areas. For example, one evening a government official was asked to introduce the guests at a benefit performance. He rose and said words to the effect, "I feel like the fifth husband of a famous movie star, on their wedding night. I know what's expected of me. The problem is how to make it interesting." That's our problem, too, isn't it? Career education is a great program. We know what's expected of us. Now—how can we make it interesting?

Summary

Although sponsored by the United States Office of Education, the career education concept cannot succeed unless it is espoused by those of us who consider ourselves educators. It is up to us to bring it into our schools through curricular changes, and it is the administrators who must take the initiative and program these changes into the schools. Assistance will be forthcoming from the Office of Education; a great deal of money has been and is being spent to develop curricular materials on all grade levels.

To prepare your school's Career Education Program, first establish a committee including yourself, one or two other administrators, your guidance counselors, teachers, and if you so desire, students and parents.

Follow-up studies of your graduates or members of the community (if yours is a new school) are essential, as is a survey of the local job market. Next you would need a survey of your present program, which you should obtain from your administrators, counselors, and teachers. From this material, your committee would develop a tentative program which would be presented to the school board, the parents, and the community.

As many teachers as possible should be involved in both the temporary and permanent planning committees. They should develop a curriculum suitable for your school. It may be developed from the one to be found in Part Two of this book, modified, of course, to suit the needs of your students.

It is important, too, to have the acceptance and active enthusiasm of the teachers. By having a specific curriculum that they have developed, by holding workshops, by doing demonstration lessons, by having resource materials, the anxieties of the teachers can be alleviated, and their enthusiasm developed. This will be a tremendous factor in the success of your Career Education Program.

3

Deciding the Form Your Career Education Program Will Take—Staffing It, and Suiting It to the Needs of Your Community

Once you have gotten past the initial acceptance of the program and are beginning to formulate a permanent one, you will want to establish two committees to work on the problems that will have to be solved. We suggest you establish a Career Education Research Committee and a Career Education Selection Committee. *The functions of the Research Committee are as follows:*

a. To decide on the form your program will take. (This is far simpler in the elementary school than in either the junior or senior high school.)

b. To survey the job opportunities in your community, in neighboring areas, and in the nation as a whole.

c. To make the adjustments your program should include to suit it to the needs of the students you serve.

This committee will probably consist of many of the people who served on the Career Education Investigation Committee. However, it should be opened up, so that any interested persons may participate. It should consist of your counselors, and representatives of teachers, parents, and students interested in the program, and in doing research and compiling data.

The functions of the second committee, the Career Education Selection Committee, will be to consider the results of studies brought in and the recommendations made by the Research Committee. They will then be in a position to make decisions in regard to the form your Career Education Program would take. This Selection Committee should consist of school board members, administrators, parents, teachers, and students. They will have to decide on the manner in which career education is to be presented to the students, the amount of class time to be spent, the budgetary allotments for implementing the program, the manner in which the program should be initiated, and the time it should begin.

As you have already realized, Career Education is a series of concepts that will be interpreted differently by each school board and, indeed, possibly by each school. We will consider many of the aspects it may take, offering to you a variety of situations from which you may select those that fit the needs and interests of both your students and your community.

THE IDEAL CAREER EDUCATION PROGRAM

The ideal program will be discussed first: That is, of course, the comprehensive educational program that begins in grade I or earlier, and continues through the young adult years. For elementary and secondary education, the program includes a restructuring of basic subjects, grades 1-12, around the theme of career development, including opportunities and requirements in the world of work. The basic academic subjects, such as mathematics, science, social studies, and language arts become more relevant because the student is helped to see the relationship to future career goals. In the elementary school, students are informed about the wide range of jobs in our economic system and the associated societal roles. In junior high school, students will explore specific clusters of occupations through hands-on experiences and field observations, as well as classroom instruction. In senior high school, students will prepare for both entry jobs (through classroom, laboratory, and cooperative educational activities) and for further education. Placement in a job or in further education are options open to every student!

A student preparing for postsecondary education while in high school would have less time for in-depth occupational preparation. Nevertheless, as a participant in a Career Education Program, he would acquire entry-level skills through some courses in school and possible through on-the-job or work center experience.

It is important that each student master the skills he will require in order to earn a living. Whether these skills are labeled "academic" or "vocational" is beside the point. The essential need is that every student be equipped to live his life as a fulfilled human being. If he is to live his life with machines, he must know how to use them. If he is to live with a slide rule or a computer, he must understand its magic. If he is to combat diseases that afflict mankind, he must know a great deal about the human body and mind and all the ills they are heir to.[1]

Obviously, putting a career education program such as this into action requires a profound restructuring of the curriculum. The ideal situation is to develop a full curriculum for all grades—from first through twelfth. This would, of course, require a long period of time. You will find a basic program outlined in the second section of this book. School board members and the general public will have to make some fundamental decisions; the Career Education Program will require additional funding for additional staff, in-service training, new equipment, new curricular materials, and other expenses. This could increase your school budget fairly substantially the first few years. However, after a school system has retooled and converted to a career education program, the continuing costs of its maintenance and operation should decline nearly to previous levels.[2]

There are times when the terms "career education" and "vocational education" are used interchangeably; however, they are not synonymous. Career education is a far broader program that encompasses vocational education. Vocational education has been and is important in that it offers the student a large number of experiences and opportunities in choosing his or her life's work. It has been with us a long time, and many people have benefited immeasurably from vocational education. However it is far more limited than career education.

The program we have outlined is, of course, an ideal program which would require much time and effort to develop and implement. However, it can be begun segment by segment, and put together as time and circumstances permit. With this in mind, let us look at the various parts of the total picture.

CAREER EDUCATION IN THE ELEMENTARY SCHOOL

The keynote is awareness—building an awareness, in the mind of the child, of the careers that are open to him, and of his own personality in relation to the world of work.

---

[1] Career Education; Description and Goals. Division of Vocational and Technical Ed. USOE, Washington.

[2] Ibid.

Career development should begin early in the life of a child and should be a developmental process continuing over many years. Career choice is that part of the process involving many choices and decisions over an extended period of time. Rarely is a career choice made at a particular time. *A young person will ultimately grow into his vocation. It is for this reason that the introduction he gets during his formative elementary school years is tremendously important.*

Ideally career awareness should be done through exploration. The child should be offered a variety of experiences encompassing every career cluster.

The United States Office of Education has divided the world of work into fifteen career or occupational clusters. We will be referring to them time and again. They are:

Agri-business and Natural Resources
Business and Office
Communication and Media
Construction
Consumer and Homemaking Education
Environment
Fine Arts and Humanities
Health
Hospitality and Recreation
Manufacturing
Marketing and Distribution
Marine Science
Personal Services
Public Service
Transportation

It is most important that the school's program be student-centered, designed to meet the needs of the individual students.

It is suggested that careers be studied in terms of the existing curriculum in the schools. If, for example, the class is doing a unit on "My City" in social studies, the various career areas to be found in the city may easily be brought in. The same is true in every subject area. The class would do research, of course. There are special techniques that may be used quite effectively in this type of work. They will be found in detail in Part Two.

Your teachers need to plan for these changes in the curriculum. Planning requires time, and it is our fervent hope that time can be allotted to them for the purpose of sitting down and working out specific lessons which will bring in the study of careers.

As can be easily seen, this type of curricular change is not terribly difficult to initiate; nor is it very expensive. As the children progress through school, the material to be covered becomes a bit more complex, but not inordinately so. Many of the careers in the career clusters can be introduced to the youngsters.

The major breakthrough involves getting the study of both careers and self into the curriculum and into the classroom. In spite of the simplicity, much is to be gained by this. If classwork is related to the study of careers, and if the young person is able to see the relevance of what he is learning, discipline problems will become lessened. Many of the latter are caused by the failure of the teacher to relate what he is teaching to the child's life. What could be more relevant than a study of careers—with the major stress being that someday, "You, Johnny, are going to have to make a living! And you are going to have to decide on a career. Which one will suit you best?"

In Chapter 5 you will learn where to write for free materials so that, even if funding is an extremely severe problem, you can still initiate a Career Education Program in the elementary school.

CAREER EDUCATION IN THE JUNIOR HIGH SCHOOL

In the junior high school it is recommended the youngsters study in depth three of the career cluster areas. These are the three they have shown the most interest in, and it is from one of these that they will choose the area in which they will be trained in entry skills in the tenth grade.

Junior high schools were originally established to provide a period of exploration for the youngsters, and the home economics and industrial shops worked on exactly that premise—which is really career education. However, now we are seeking to expand the introduction to "hands-on" experiences in many more areas than just these two.

Here, again, the learning of language arts, mathematics, sciences, and social studies in the abstract, without practical application, has limited students' abilities to find meaning and relevance in their school work. The present system that emphasizes abstract reasoning has been particularly detrimental to those youngsters whose strengths are other than in the abstract, verbal, and quantitative areas. It has so separated academic learning at all levels of education from reality that even those students who reject the "establishment" do so without the practical skills necessary to bring about the change they see as essential.

Schools that restructure and focus basic subject areas around the career development theme will be able to capitalize on what interests and motivates the student. Basic skills will become useful tools in reaching the goals set by students because they will be able to identify career interests to which they may relate their education.

Redirecting basic subject areas to include career development objectives will provide the basis for activity-centered learning and permit laboratory application for abstract basic skills.[3]

But now let us pose a question. Supposing your junior high youngsters have never had the career and self-awareness material which is part of the program for the elementary school. It would be necessary to cover this, although not in as great detail as it would have been covered in six years of work in the lower grades. However, the objectives of those years would have to be taken into consideration before the junior high school program can go into effect. It is based on the assumption that the career awareness stage has already been reached and, indeed, passed.

Possibly the best way to do this is through a year-long course in the study of occupations given in the seventh grade. This course should be geared to the fifteen career clusters, so that the work in the eighth and ninth grades would be a continuation in the same framework. Covered in a course in Occupations, are an awareness of the wide variety of careers available and the development of the concept that a person's wants and needs, likes and dislikes, must be considered in the choice of a life's work.

There is no reason for the junior high school administrator to feel that "We can't use the Career Education Program. Our children haven't been prepared by the elementary schools." Rather, he or she must see this as a need to catch up. Since the eighth and ninth years take the same materials, in greater depth, with more emphasis on the actual "hands-on" experiences, the overview in the seventh grade is very valuable because it allows the pupils to build a framework or background.

Far too many children and young people are totally ignorant of many of the most basic concepts in regard to careers and career choice. If we are to work with them, they must be brought up from the beginning. It goes without saying, of course, that this would be done on the level of the students' comprehension.

---

[3]Career Education: Description and Goals' Division of Vocational and Technical Education, Bureau of Adult, Vocational and Technical Education, U.S. Office of Education, Washington, D.C., 1971, p. 4.

Hands-on experiences may be structured for the junior high student in a number of ways involving both the community and the parents. They may work as volunteers in local industries or businesses. They may be placed in the working environment for a period of time without actually working. They may visit various establishments to interview people working there, or they may listen to speakers from different career areas. The students may be given further experiences in the world of work by being given the responsibility of making their own arrangements for these activities. (The school would, of course, have done the preliminary structuring, so the students' mission is known to the persons whom they contact.)

CAREER EDUCATION IN THE SENIOR HIGH SCHOOL

It is the senior high schools that must carry the bulk of the change into effect, if we, as a nation, are to accept career education. It is hoped that the student will have had exploratory experiences in the junior high school, and that these experiences, in turn, will provide the student with knowledge to assist in decision-making in the high school regarding areas of study and more specific preparation which the student will pursue in senior high school (and possibly postsecondary and adult programs). Guidance and counseling are important to aid the student in developing his decision-making abilities.

All persons completing secondary school will be prepared to exercise two basic options—immediate employment and/or further education. This requires a curriculum that offers every student in secondary school the opportunity to develop a marketable skill. Emphasis will be given to the basic communication and computational skills necessary for a broad range of gainful employment and educational opportunities. Additionally, each student will be equipped with at least minimal job entry level skills in one of the career clusters. This will be accomplished in a variety of ways, including but not limited to: (1) enrollment in vocational education programs, (2) work experiences in the community, or (3) participation in some other occupational education experience.

Some students will elect not to pursue further education immediately after completing secondary school. These students will be provided an in-depth vocational education program to develop their knowledge and skills in a family of occupations within a career cluster. (For example: air pollution abatement and control are within the environment cluster; fashion merchandising is within the marketing and distribution cluster.) Basic knowledge essential to performing in other families of occupations within the cluster will also be acquired by each student. Relationships of families within the cluster and between clusters wil be explored so that students will continuously be aware of additional opportunities available. They will be encouraged to pursue the necessary further education as their occupational aspirations broaden. It is essential, therefore, for students in a vocational education program to be equipped with the academic skills essential to the pursuit of further education in the field of their career interest.

Each senior high school student will receive the following kinds of experiences:

1. A "core" curriculum in the occupational cluster of his choice. This core curriculum will build upon the exploratory and entry-level skill development experiences at the junior high level and will provide higher levels of skill development when these skills are common to all the occupations in the cluster. Students preparing for job entry and students preparing for higher education would be enrolled in the cluster curriculum.

2. Basic subject matter areas such as language arts, social studies, mathematics, and science which are related to and which support the cluster core curriculum selected by the student.

3. A choice of electives designed specifically for job preparation and/or a choice of electives designed specifically to prepare for entry into further education in an area of his choice.

Consequently, all persons completing secondary school will be prepared to exercise two basic options—immediate employment and/or further education.

An attempt will be made to provide some work experience for all students at some time during their secondary school enrollment. Arrangements will be entered into with business, industry, and other employers for the purpose of providing students with entry-level skills. Continued emphasis will be given to cooperative vocational education as one effective method of providing in-depth training for occupations.

Many students will choose to prepare for further education while in secondary school. These students will have limited time for in-depth occupational preparation. Minimal job entry-level skills will be developed by these students through the cluster program and the technique of work experience as previously discussed, or through participation in some other occupational education experience.[4]

STAFFING WILL DEPEND ON BUDGETARY ALLOWANCES

Every person in the school system has a role to play in career education. School board members, administrators, teachers, counselors, nurses, librarians, paraprofessionals, aides, and students can contribute to an effective program. The cooperation of community members is absolutely vital to the success of this program—from the trips made by the elementary school pupils to the neighborhood bakery to the jobs supplied by local industrialists.

The services of the counselors are extremely important if the Career Education Program is to be effective. A ratio of 300 pupils to one counselor is well worth striving for, particularly on the junior and senior high school levels.

Because of many of the activities involved, extra personnel are needed to work with the students in small groups. Team teaching may be used, provided the discussion groups are kept to less than ten children. Since the entire community becomes the classroom, assistance is needed while taking the youngsters on trips. This might involve paraprofessionals or aides. An excellent source of auxiliary personnel is a local college. The services of students, particularly those studying to be teachers, can be very beneficial to both the school and the would-be teachers.

In the high school, as academic courses are replaced by skills courses, a change of personnel will be required. Many of the people qualified to teach the skill courses will not be professional teachers. Nevertheless their services will be necessary if the students are really to be trained for the world of work.

The person who coordinates the entire program can really influence its success. Try to find a person who becomes involved, who cares, and who can throw himself or herself into it. There is so much work to be done—arrangements to be made, materials to be obtained, people to be contacted. He or she must put forth the philosophy of the program and its application. He or she must be available to give assistance to any teachers or other staff members who require it. When selecting this person, make sure he is someone who truly, without reservations, believes in the concept of career education.

---

[4]Career Education: Description and Goals.

Without question this person needs clerical help. There are many, many letters to be written and phone calls to be made. If he or she tries to do it, valuable time is lost.

It will be the function of the Career Education Research Committee to consider the various programs possible and to report, at the proper time, to the Selection Committee with their findings.

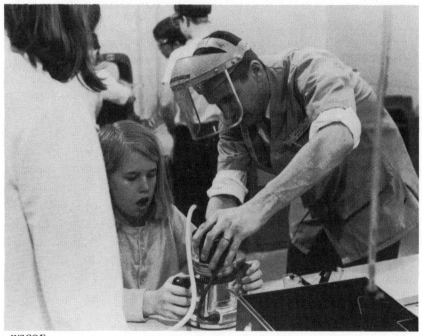

WSCOE

INVOLVING THE PEOPLE, THE BUSINESSES, AND THE INSTITUTIONS OF THE COMMUNITY IN YOUR PROGRAM

Business and labor leaders have already been active in some specialized fields of education. Industry advisory committees have been helpful in planning programs in newly emerging occupational areas or evaluating and upgrading programs in the established occupations and crafts. Representatives from business and labor should be approached on two levels: (1) for general support of the program, and (2) for their expertise in a specific industry or a particular occupational field. It should be self-evident that any program concerned with education for a career must make provisions for active participation by persons familiar with the industrial and labor relations process and with the skill requirements of particular occupations. Of equal importance is the role industry can play in providing the students with opportunities to observe working situations or engage in actual employment.

One of the faults of many educators has been that they have never worked outside the walls of a school building. How can they possibly present as accurate a picture as the person who has been employed in the situation, or who hires personnel or supervises them?

A key feature of career education is that it can provide service by the students to the community whenever and wherever such services provide a useful learning experience. The cooperation of the school and the members of the community cannot help but bring about a better community.

Besides the local business and industrial personnel, there is a large source of valuable assistance available in the senior citizen population. These men and women with careers behind them represent a rich and valuable resource that can and should be used fully. Many of these senior citizens have mastered crafts that are in short supply. Others have skills in the use of tools, materials, and processes that are no longer practiced in the labor market, but can serve as a basis for children and young people to learn important job skills and recreational or leisure time activities.

Another source of assistance in the Career Education Program can be the service clubs in your locality. Because the members represent many occupations and careers, the clubs can often supply speakers and possibly teachers. Furthermore, service clubs are always seeking opportunities to serve the community and youth in particular.

You may find it advisable to put out a newsletter periodically (once a month or so) describing the activities going on in the school—and especially describing its work with outside agencies, citing those that should be credited. Every individual needs recognition—and businesses and industries, like schools, are composed of individuals.

SUITING YOUR PROGRAM TO FIT
THE NEEDS OF YOUR STUDENTS

The surveys that follow are all to be done by the Career Education Research Committee.

Surveying the Industries in the Community
to Determine Where the Job Opportunities Are

This task has previously been done by the counselors—particularly for guiding and structuring the programs in the junior and senior high schools. In the words of Professor Robert Hoppock of New York University, "The counselor should put his hat on his head" and go out to visit businesses and industries—to find out, first hand, what their requirements for workers are. Personnel managers very often will describe the specific job opportunities available. When it is deemed of value, they may be invited to speak—either to adults (the school board, the parents, or the faculty) or to the students. They can point out the education or training needed, and indicate to the students where they may obtain it.

Other sources of such information are the local labor union offices. In addition to pointing out where there are job opportunities, the union officials can discuss any apprenticeship programs they offer. These programs are extremely important if a young person is interested in learning one of the skills such as electrical work, plumbing, or lithography. There are many, many more apprenticeship programs available. The apprenticeship offers years of combined work and study for the high school graduate, enabling him to earn a salary that increases as he becomes more proficient.

The Role of the United States Employment Service
in Determining Which Career Areas
Require Trained Personnel

The local branch of the U.S.E.S. is able to offer to the school a great deal of current information in regard to a large variety of job opportunities.* Since employers are constantly in touch with the U.S.E.S. personnel, they really have their fingers on the pulse of the career opportunity situation. In many offices a new system called the Job Information Service (J.I.S.) is being established which has, as an integral part, a job bank. This bank is a daily, computerized listing of all jobs available. There is also a library where prospective employees can get information in regard to the jobs being offered. There are plans for the J.I.S. to be installed in 150 major metropolitan areas. The counselor and committee upon obtaining copies of the job bank listings, can work with these statistics and are thereby able to

---

*It is referred to by the name of the state. For instance, New York State Employment Service.

recommend courses to the Selection Committee that are needed in the community and nearby areas.

Surveying the Nearest Large Cities for Career Opportunities

The State Employment Services will be an important source for this information, as discussed previously.

A further source is the help-wanted columns of newspapers in neighboring communities and in the metropolitan areas nearby. Since many young people must move to metropolitan areas to find employment, the courses that your school offers should take this into consideration. High schools in Massachusetts, for example, are giving courses in data processing, optical technology, basic and advanced electronics, instrumentation, automotive machinist, machine design, hydraulics, precision sheet metal, and others. The introduction of these courses necessitated a revision of the mathematics and science programs. Algebra, geometry, trigonometry, physics, chemistry, and solid geometry, when applicable, should induce motivation by the use of a relationship to a technical major subject.[5]

The help-wanted columns, too, can be used by the teachers as part of their lessons. They will serve as motivation for many of the young people. Often, when the students are able to actually see the need for trained personnel and the fact that they are being prepared to fill that need they become far more involved in their educations.

Checking with Professional Organizations in Regard to the Need for Professionals in Your Community or in Neighboring Ones

The need for teachers was a very pressing one until the beginning of the 1970s. Then the situation changed greatly, and, with the decreased birth rate, continues to change. Teachers are still required to replace those who are retiring, being promoted, or who leave the profession for any other reason, but the number of teachers needed is far less than it was five or so years ago. Some professions have a distinct lack of personnel—such as nursing. (That is true at the time of this writing. It may change tomorrow. Counselors must keep on top of this situation.) Professional organizations can give informa-

---

[5]Move (Massachusetts Opportunities in Vocational Education), Blue Hills Regional Technical School, Canton, Massachusetts. Division of Occ. Ed., State of Massachusetts, p. 4.

tion in regard to the number of career opportunities in the entire nation as well. This factor, too, should be taken into consideration in your planning, since not every graduate will look for employment in your area. However, estimates of future needs may be incorrect and should be considered with a grain of salt.

With this in mind, consideration of publications is important. The professional journals and magazines, such as the *Vocational Guidance Quarterly,* contain a wealth of material. Organizations such as the American Personnel and Guidance Association's National Career Information Center put out materials such as *Inform,* a monthly brochure of career topics. Private groups, such as the Federation of Jewish Philanthropies Personnel and Guidance Service publish a newsletter that emphasizes current career opportunities in the New York area which it services. All of this is the type of information with which the counselor has been dealing for years. The difference is that now it is to be utilized by far more students than ever before—because it is to be brought to them in their classes as well as in the guidance office.

Careers in Civil Service

The largest employer in the nation is the government—be it Federal, state or city. Because of this, we feel it is extremely important that civil service careers be taken into consideration when you are planning your program. The needs for certain occupations are ever present and by training pupils for them, more effective, efficient service is possible. Some of the up-and-coming career areas—such as consumer science and environmental science—are in government service. Furthermore, many students may be interested in working for the Federal government in other parts of the country.

Using the Information You Have Obtained
to the Best Advantage

When the Career Education Research Committee has completed its study, it may use the following form to tabulate its information:

1. In what careers are there the most job opportunities in your immediate area? What statistics is this based on?
2. For which of these do you offer preparation?
3. What type of preparation?
   a. For entry jobs
   b. For further education

4. What are the career areas offering some (but a considerably smaller) number of job opportunities in your area? What statistics is this based on?

5. For which of these do you offer preparation?

6. What type of preparation?

    a. For entry jobs

    b. For further education

7. In what careers are there the most job opportunities within 250 miles of your community? What statistics is this based on?

8. For which of these do you offer preparation?

9. What type of preparation?

    a. For entry jobs

    b. For further education

10. On a nationwide scale, for what careers are there *now* the most job opportunities? What statistics is this based on?

11. For which of these do you offer preparation?

.12. What type of preparation?

    a. For entry jobs

    b. For further education

When this survey is completed, you have a picture of the career opportunities that are available currently and which will probably be available to your graduates. Of course, career opportunities do change. You are no doubt familiar with the aerospace industry, and with the teaching profession. However, these are exceptions to the rule. We know, without question, that we are living in a technological society, and that, though there are variations, roads in career study must be toward training skilled individuals—be they skilled craftsmen, technicians, or professionals.

Using the statistics you have put together, you can then present to your Career Education Selection Committee a series of courses from which they can select those that will best suit the needs of your students and your community.

These results should be taken into consideration in determining the program in any school, on any level. While it is important to learn about as many different careers as possible, even children in the first six grades should be shown the job opportunities part of the picture. In the junior high their experiential learning should come from the prevailing industries for the most part. In the senior high school most, if not all of your career cluster courses, should be in areas in which there are job opportunities—so that, upon graduation, those students who wish to begin their careers immediately may do so.

Summary

In order to decide on the form your Career Education Program should take, it is suggested a research committee be created to study the situation. Staffing the program will depend on the grade level of your school, and the manner in which the program should operate. However, community members, parents, people from business and industry, and even students from local colleges should be asked to participate. To decrease the load of the teachers, paraprofessionals, and aides, college student assistants can be employed.

To develop a program that will be suited to the needs of your particular community, a study should be conducted by the Research Committee. They should survey the industries in the locality to determine where the job opportunities are. The United States Employment Service should be consulted; the help-wanted columns of newspapers should be reviewed; and the professional organizations in the area consulted. Careers in civil service—Federal, state or city—should be taken into consideration.

When this information has been gathered, a report should be prepared by the Research Committee with recommendations based on the information obtained. The Selection Committee then has the basis for deciding on the program your school will adopt.

4

How to Motivate and Train the Staff Involved in the Career Education Program

With career education, as with any program that is to be taught to children, if the teachers are not involved and enthusiastic, the program is next to worthless. It is absolutely essential that the staff be deeply committed to this type of education. For this reason we have suggested including as many teachers as wish to be included in the planning stages of the program. They must believe in what they are teaching and they must present it to the young people with all of the verve they can muster. (In this respect this is no different, from any other type of good teaching.) Then the students must take an active part in the learning process.

The basic philosophy of career education must become part of the teacher's background. He or she must realize exactly how important the information and experiences the children will get in career education are, and how much these can influence the young people's future lives. Career education must become part and parcel of the regular school work.

"But how will I find the time for it?" the conscientious elementary school teacher asks. Let us answer that right now.

1. As you teach children the reading skills, is there any reason they cannot be reading material about careers?

2. As they learn the skills that will enable them to speak properly, can they not be reporting on careers?

3. As they write compositions, can they not write about careers?

More important, though, is the fact that the conscientious teacher must be shown that this information is so important that it deserves its own priority. Suggestions have been made that, as a student studies science, careers in that field will be brought to his attention. The same is true of every subject area—that the occupations to be found within it be added at some point to the units of work already in existence. The Career Education Program has been called by the Center for Vocational and Technical Education at Ohio State University, which is in charge of developing career education models, "a bridge to reality." This bridge connects schooling with the world of work. The Center has been charged with the responsibility for the overall development of a school-based Career Education Model for the U.S. Office of Education. Nearly 100 curriculum units are in the process of being revised, pilot tested, and field tested. Teachers will be able to obtain and use such materials. However, the materials expert teachers will develop for use with their own classes will be worthy of attention as well. Career education must be a product of the thinking of everyone in the education profession. The techniques that follow are suggested for experimentation in your Career Education Program.

USING THE INFORMAL GROUP SITUATION

Career education should be presented to the children and young adults with an entirely new basis that will make it different from previous courses. The use of the informal group situation, the "open classroom" approach, can work exceptionally well for this material since it offers the student a chance to sample and to choose the areas in which he is primarily interested.

Let us say that for career education, the classroom is set up with many reading and research materials around the room. In addition to this, the use of instruments, the "tools of the trade"—be they stethoscopes or hammers, hygrometers or slide rules, should be added for further experimentation. The pupils should have the opportunity to handle equipment and to read about the various occupations as well. We believe working within the fifteen career clusters suggested by the Office of Education (of Health, Education and Welfare) is effective and will use this approach in the curriculum portion of this book.

This technique will require ingenuity and creativity on the part of the teacher, who may also use some of the other methods that will be outlined later. Career education is not for just one group of students or another, but encompasses all groups—and therefore will broaden the knowledge of each person studying it. How many women (even those who drive cars) know what a carburetor is? Yet shouldn't they—even if they don't repair their own automobiles? People love to do things—witness the huge number of do-it-yourself projects—and this form of education allows for much exploration in much the same manner.

Where does the teacher obtain that carburetor? The answer is so simple it is almost unbelievable. Ask the youngsters—and, almost without question, one will be forthcoming. It might not be so easy to obtain a computer but, here again, ingenuity will provide an answer. If you cannot obtain one, you can visit one.

If a true "open classroom" situation is adopted with several classes participating, the need to duplicate the materials is eliminated as students wander through the rooms. This is the opportunity to experiment with the "open" approach for a very valid reason. Books, audio-visual materials, and equipment may be utilized by many groups of children.

Muriel S. Karlin, Board of Education, City of New York

TRIPS

Trips are an absolutely essential aspect of career education for they place the students on-the-spot, right where it's happening. They are able to experience the sights, smells, sounds, and pressures of particular occupations.

One class was taken on a trip to a photographic laboratory. It was a modern plant, but the odor of chemicals was very strong. One youngster said to his teacher, "I used to think I wanted to be a photographer, but I can't take that smell." Another child said, "I could never work in a place like this." When questioned, she gave her reasons. "There are no windows, and I feel I couldn't work in a place where I could never see the sun."

Trips involve a variety of experiences. The visitor is able to observe not one, but a number of people performing their duties. A trip to a hospital, for example, can offer the opportunity of studying almost an entire cluster of health careers.

When taking the youngsters on trips, there are two types possible:

General observation to see people working in as many occupations as possible. This is the broad, overall view, and is excellent as the basis for introductory material.

Specific observation to see what one or two careers involve on a minute-to-minute, day-to-day basis. What does the person actually do? How often does he do it? What instruments or equipment does he have to use?

For general observations, entire classes may be taken on trips. For specific observation, it is far better to take small groups of youngsters who have manifested interest in a particular occupation. These small groups may be escorted by aides or paraprofessionals.

For whichever type of trip, there should be a work sheet prepared in advance by the pupils with the help of the teacher. It should list:

1. What the aim of the trip is. (In other words, what we are going to see.)

2. What information are we trying to obtain from this trip?
    a. What are the working conditions?
    b. What are the educational or vocational requirements?
    c. What are the salaries?
    d. Would I like any of these careers? Why or why not?

If the youngsters are doing a career survey, which will be described subsequently, they will have many more questions to answer since they will talk with people they meet while on the trip.

INVITING PARENTS OR COMMUNITY MEMBERS TO
SPEAK TO OR TEACH THE CLASS

One of the logical outcomes and one of the objectives of career education is the involvement of members of the community. It begins with a request for a parent to speak to the members of his youngster's class and progresses to the point where parents or community members are teaching mini-courses and giving lectures in their areas of expertise.

We have already quoted elementary school principal Richard Erskine of Steward Elementary School, Puyallup, Washington. He claims one of the highest ratios of parent involvement anywhere in the state. They volunteer to teach skill classes such as typing, carpentry, and electricity. This is not just to let the students fool around with equipment, he explains, "but to teach the skill and study about the jobs that go with those skills."[1]

Career education is a means of bringing together the people who need this education (our children) with people who can offer it to them—straight from the horse's mouth—in this case the professions, business and industry.

When a career cluster is being studied and the class is asked, "Is there anyone who knows a person in one of these careers?" generally hands will go up. If not, there is always the coordinator to contact.

It is one of the coordinator's provinces to be able to contact individuals who are interested and willing to take part in the program.

Speakers may be asked to address small or large groups. It should be impressed upon them that, though a group may be small, it is composed of young people who are actually deeply interested in that career area. (Incidentally, the young people must be prepared to hear the speaker and the correct mode of behavior impressed very firmly upon them. Nothing brings adverse publicity as strongly upon a school as a guest's being badly received.)

Speakers should be asked to bring with them as many of their tools and other equipment as possible—and to make their discussion practical and to the point. If they are willing to allow the handling of

---

[1] What about Vocational Education? Washington State Coordinating Council for Occupational Education. Olympia, Washington, 98504. Sept. 1971.

their equipment by the young people, this is certainly to be desired. No one expects a musician to allow the kids to touch a Stradivarius, but if he can bring a violin they can handle, so much the better.

Speakers very often become the contacts for supplying jobs for students and for supplying experiences within actual places of

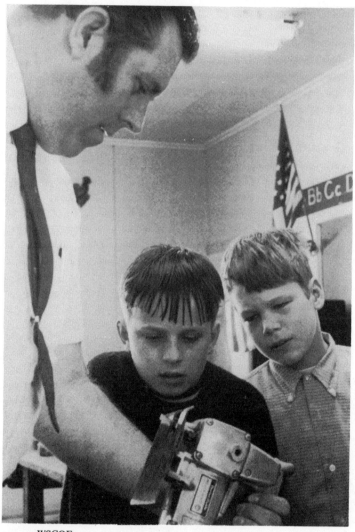

WSCOE

business. They should be brought into the school situation first by being asked to speak in order to establish a bridge between them and the school. This may be followed up by sending the pupils on trips, and then by requests for part-time or "sampling" jobs.

COMMITTEE WORK

One of the most effective ways to combine the open classroom situation with career study is through committee work. Even very young children can benefit by working together.

In setting up committee work, be sure the questions the committee must answer and the work it must do are outlined very clearly; assist the class in dividing up the work so that no child is overloaded.

You may wish to have your committees work on assembly programs in which they describe and illustrate as graphically as possible the work particular careers entail. They may do these in the form of radio or television programs. "You Are There," for example, is an excellent device for showing what a coal miner actually does as he pursues his occupation.

Your committees may work on bulletin board displays, again showing the various tasks that go into the working day of a person in a specific career. Another type of bulletin board display might include many of the careers in one of the career clusters. Still another type of work for a committee might be "Careers that come from hobbies." Such areas as photography, stamp-selling, music, or sports might be considered.

Committees may work on plays and dramatizations for such situations as job interviews or stories of "My day on the job." Committees may also make up games involving careers. (There are a number of commercially available games that might be used as models.)

A collage made by a group of youngsters can be very effective, particularly when they handle a topic such as "Careers that keep you out-of-doors" or "Careers that supply the food we eat." Murals, too, can be developed with similar purposes in mind.

Establishing committees where children seem to share interests in particular careers is one way in which this technique may be used. Another is to group young people with a variety of occupational interests, so that these interests may be shared.

INDIVIDUALIZING INSTRUCTION
AND WORKING WITH EACH CHILD

One of the huge objectives of the Career Education Program is to develop self-awareness on the part of each student. We hope to help the child see himself as a human being who is unique and who has special talents, interests, and abilities. We hope to help him utilize these in his choice of a career. It is therefore our task to help him find not one but many career areas that will suit him, as an individual. He will then have a choice of careers available to him.

By offering the child the opportunity to be introduced to many occupations, and giving him the chance to select those he wishes to study further, we are providing such individualization. Counseling should be available, as the child matures, to assist him in learning about himself.

As a child selects a career, by working with him, by asking him, "What is it about this career that interested you?" by helping him to understand why he selected it, we are able to bring out factors the child may never see by himself. By reviewing with him the information he gathers, by helping him with his career studies, by offering to him chances to see and handle equipment, we help his development into a human being who is capable of thinking about himself in terms of careers.

The tools of the counselor will hopefully be made available to every child who requires them—the interest inventories, the aptitude and the ability tests. These, too, help the youngster to determine his career orientations.

It is extremely important that no career be given a negative connotation. There is a huge variety of occupations, all of which are worthy of consideration if they suit the individual. It would be a grievous error to point to any career with derision. Not every one can be a brain surgeon, nor would everyone be happy with the tremendous amount of responsibility this entails. It is for the child to judge his area—not for the teacher. It is for the teacher to introduce as many areas as possible, so that the child can see that there are not one or two but literally thousands of careers from which he can select.

By giving each child a choice of the projects on which he can work, by allowing him to select his own area, by developing his knowledge of careers as much as possible, we are able to expand horizons of children who have never had such opportunities before.

This is especially true of disadvantaged children, who often have had relatively few experiences in connection with the world of work.

USE OF THE INTERVIEW
TO LEARN ABOUT VARIOUS CAREERS

A further example of individualization in regard to career study is the interview. This device offers a one-to-one exchange of information. It provides the child with the opportunity to learn about a career from a person practicing it.

Children may be instructed to interview their parents and other members of the community. It is essential that, when this tool is used, they be given specific questions. The youngsters will be seeking different types of information, depending on the grade they are in and the topic they are investigating. Work out the list of questions with your class, getting specific questions from them; but do not rely on the youngsters' memories. Put the list on the board to be copied into their notebooks or place it on a rexograph master and ditto it.

A child in the first grade may interview his mother to learn what tasks she does in the course of her day. (This often comes as an eye opener. Adults have knowledge about the many and varied things the mother does, but children are not usually aware of them.)

He may certainly interview his father. (This is important, in view of the fact that there are junior high school students who do not know their fathers' occupations.)

People who have been in their occupations at least ten years can be interviewed to find out how technology and science have changed their work. (In dentistry, for example, the high speed drill has had a tremendous effect on saving the dentist's time and the patient's discomfort.)

It may be necessary to have interviews arranged. This is the function of the coordinator's office. In every school that offers career education there should be some person who assists in this aspect of the work. The interview is a most important tool and its effectiveness should not be left to chance. Community members are usually very willing to be interviewed. This is a case of putting the children in touch with the right people and it should be done as often and as simply as possible. Of course this does not mean every child will be interviewing someone once a week. There will be times when the interviews can be set up by the youngster himself. But, when needed, the coordinator's office should offer this service.

THE CORRECT USE OF PRINTED MATERIALS
AS A BASIS FOR DISCUSSION

There are many ways in which printed materials may serve as a basis for discussion. When studying occupations, because there are so many and varied careers, it is efficient to have individuals or groups of children read about different careers and present their findings to the class. This can range from "I learned the shipfitter is a person who lays out the position of various parts of a ship, such as . . ." to "The nuclear physicist is the person who . . . ". This will, of course, depend on the grade level and sophistication of the youngsters. The presentations may be in the form of individual or group reports, panel discussions, or class discussions. They may also be in the form of games, such as "I Have a Secret Occupation."

There are other ways the material may be presented. It may be dramatized, with the children acting out the parts in plays they have written. These may be radio or television broadcasts, for example. They may also do role-playing in which they act out, spontaneously, the various activities within a given career, basing this on information they have learned from their reading.

In considering information gained from reading, there are several important items to note.

1. Is the material current? If it is more than five years old, it should be checked and rechecked carefully.

2. What is the attitude of the author? Is it favorable? (Generally it is.) Did he like the career? *Was he personally engaged in it?*

3. What is the author's attitude in regard to women in the particular occupation? It is important for children to understand that career opportunities for women are increasing.

Many of us are used to taking the printed page as if it were the gospel truth. In career education we cannot do this. Printed material is a tool, but only one of many that we have at our disposal.

THE USE OF AUDIO-VISUAL MATERIALS

There is a wealth of available material of this type—particularly films and filmstrips. In the chapter on establishing the media center this will be discussed in detail. However, there are several points we wish to make here. One is that this material must be current for it to be of maximum use. Even material a few years old may be outdated.

Another factor to consider is that some of the films and filmstrips may be propaganda. If this is so they should be discussed with the youngsters viewing them. There are times when careers are presented entirely in a favorable light, which may be very unrealistic, and this must be taken into consideration.

For the two reasons mentioned, we suggest all films, filmstrips, and other audio-visual material such as cassettes be previewed or prelistened to by the coordinator of the program or people he designates to do so. If this step is omitted, you may find children coming away with ideas other than those you wish them to get. If each teacher has time to use these materials before class use, so much the better. If not, the official viewing or listening should be enough.

As with interviewing and reading, the children should have a specific purpose in using the material. This may be to familiarize them with the career and to give them an overall view of the duties involved. Films, filmstrips and cassettes may be used as motivational devices, and very often they are most effective in this area. As you introduce a new career cluster, they may be the first procedures you use to introduce the unit or they may be used as a source of information for research or reporting.

You may have the children do viewing or listening, and then have them do a critical analysis of what they have seen. This is an excellent way of having them sharpen their minds in regard to believing everything they see or hear.

You may note that there are careers that are the basis for many films, filmstrips, articles, and books. Often these are the "glamour" careers, which should be presented to the children with the concept that they are very difficult to succeed in, and that one almost always needs a "break," no matter how talented or hard working one is. Then, too, there are those careers for which it is very difficult to find any information, because they are so lacking in "glamour." When this situation is encountered, it is important to cover those careers as well—especially since they often prove to be the ones many of the young people will ultimately enter.

USING PROGRAMMED LEARNING

Still another method for the presentation of career oriented information is through the use of programmed learning. It is possible for the teacher to use programs that have already been prepared or to prepare his own. This is by no means as difficult as it sounds the first time one considers the idea.

By use of this method, children are able to work at their own pace and to concentrate on those areas in which they are really interested.

Programmed learning may also be used to teach skills such as speedwriting or bookkeeping. This is particularly useful in small school systems, where teaching entry-level jobs will present a problem. Many correspondence courses make use of this method, some of them quite successfully.

While programmed learning is often constructed so that the student learns without a great deal of assistance from the teacher, this is not necessarily true, and the combination of the program and individualized class work may prove to be very effective.

Another interesting experiment you may wish to try is to have the children construct programs. You can find instructions for this in the library, and it is a challenging interesting assignment.

THE USE OF CLOSED CIRCUIT TELEVISION IN THE CAREER EDUCATION PROGRAM

If your school is fortunate enough to have this facility at your disposal, it may be used very effectively with team teaching to bring career information to large groups of children at the same time. These groups should then be broken up into small units for discussion of the various career areas. The use of television can save many hours of teachers' time and effort. Audio-visual materials may be shown, as well as plays which the children have written and produced. (This, of course, is excellent motivation.) Interviews, reports, even trips may be conveyed to the entire group through the use of the television set.

You will find there are commercially prepared television programs in the area of careers that can be shown as part of the career education curriculum. Films, too, can be shown to the entire grade. For example, the American Hereford Foundation offers a film called "The Changing Cowboy" which traces the development of the cowboy and his method of handling cattle from the early days to the present. It shows, too, how the computer is used in this career area of cattle raising.

Particularly in the development of career awareness, the more information we can present, the better—and films by closed circuit television are an excellent means of doing this because they can be followed by a person discussing them, and then by the group discussion.

DOING A CAREER SURVEY

As the children reach the fifth and sixth grades they are capable of doing extensive research in particular career areas. We have named this "Doing a Career Survey." This consists of independent or group research, with the basic idea of having the youngster learn about a specific career in depth. This is not necessarily the career he will decide to go into, but he is learning a technique that he may use throughout his lifetime. For example, as a forty-year-old he may have to change his career because he is phased out of a job and an industry. (This, unfortunately, is far from a rare occurrence.) If he remembers how to make a career survey, he can choose a new career intelligently.

We are going to list the questions we feel should be answered when a person surveys a career. You may decide to change them or you may discuss them with your class and allow them to make the decision. The following, though, can serve as a starting-off point for your work:

1. Every career is composed of many tasks that when put together make up the career. If you were to go into this career, what exactly would you have to do on a day-to-day basis?

2. Where would you work? Would you be indoors or outdoors; would you sit, stand, or move around? Would you be in a large area, or confined to a small place?

3. What would be your dealings with other people? Would you work with them? Would you serve them? Would you be dealing with many others? Would you work with children or with senior citizens?

4. Would you be doing work that involves using your hands?

5. Would you be doing work that involves solving many problems?

6. Would you be doing work which is varied or monotonous? How would you react to this?

7. What education or training would you need to perform this career?

8. Where would you be able to get this education?

9. What is the usual starting salary for this type of work?

10. What steps would you have to take, from now until you are eligible, to prepare for this career?

When your youngsters do a career survey, it is essential that they see this as a very important piece of work. Each of the questions above may be expanded. For example, Item 2 might include such additional questions as: Is there a great deal of noise where you would work? Are there any odors? Is there excessive heat or cold?

Encourage the youngsters to find their answers to the career survey questions in as many places as possible. Here are some suggestions:

1. Probably the best way to answer career survey questions is by obtaining experience "on-the-job." If the young person can get a job, either for a salary or as a volunteer, working after school, on Saturdays, or during vacations, he can get a sample of what the career is like. This is possible, for example, when a girl becomes a "candy striper." She places herself in a hospital environment.

2. By interviewing people employed in the job. It is better to obtain information from several people than from one, who may be biased or unhappy in his work.

3. By visiting places of employment where people pursuing this career may be found.

4. By listening to speakers, and possibly questioning them after they have talked to the entire group.

5. By reading about the career. There is a great deal of information about almost every career in the form of books or periodicals. The United States Government has published several excellent sources of information. The Dictionary of Occupational Titles (known as the D.O.T.) and the Occupational Outlook Handbook are two of the most inclusive where they may obtain much of the information they need to know.

6. For finding out salaries, one of the best sources of information is the help-wanted section of the local and metropolitan newspaper.

7. Your students may contact local employment agencies for further information. This includes the local branch of the United States Employment Service, which may be listed under the name of your state, as, for example, the New York State Employment Service.

8. The school library will be a source of information, as well as the guidance office.

9. The guidance counselors should be thought of as the experts in the field of careers, and their help should be requested when information is not obtainable elsewhere.

As you can see, this career survey may be as extensive or as simple as you decide to make it; but it helps the young people to concentrate on the information they should have when they consider careers seriously.

Summary

In order to insure a successful Career Education Program, the teachers must be interested, involved, and anxious to experiment. There are a variety of techniques suggested in this chapter. These include the use of the open environment, and informal group situation; trips; and getting parents and community members involved in the program. The children benefit from doing committee work and from individualized instruction. The interviewing technique, the use of printed materials as a basis for discussion, audio-visual materials, programmed learning, and closed circuit television, are all introduced.

Methods for teaching each child to do a career survey are outlined, as well as information in regard to where he can find the answers to the survey questions. It is suggested very strongly (almost commanded) that career education be made something special.

5

How to Develop
Your Career Education Resources
Including a Multimedia Center
at Relatively Little Cost

The creation of a body of resource material, and even a multimedia center, can be done effectively and at relatively little cost if you make use of the large amount of material that is available gratis from many business or governmental organizations. A multimedia center, we believe, is both an intellectual and physical approach to solving a problem. Most schools have some audio-visual equipment and some resource material. Many schools have a great deal. By centralizing this equipment and material, by making it available to individual students as well as teachers, by developing a system for classifying it so that it is easily obtainable, by purchasing equipment easily used by students and establishing the places for them to use it, the multimedia center is created.

The role of the guidance counselor in this particular situation cannot be overestimated. Career education, to be more than merely courses in occupations, must utilize the counselor's skills in terms of helping young people to discover their talents and abilities. It should also utilize their skills in the development of the resource center.

Many counselors are able to work up excellent materials to suit the needs of the pupils within the school. This material, including questionnaires and reports, should become part of the file of permanent reference material. It should be readily available for any student or teacher to use.

WSCOE

In this chapter we are concerned with a multimedia center (or resource center) dealing with career education materials. We will be considering printed materials, films, and filmstrips (for which projectors of various kinds are necessary), tapes and recordings.

It is essential that a reliable person be put in charge of the media center. This may be a librarian, a teacher, or a counselor, but it should be a person who will take an active interest in the Career Education Program and work hard to make the center as functional and complete as possible. This may be the career education coordinator, or it may be another person who will work closely with the career education coordinator.

In every area we must stress the need for currency. Not the green kind—although that never hurts. This currency is, of course, synonymous with recency. Nothing can turn young people off as much as seeing a film from 1940—so obvious because of the clothing and hair styles. It is particuarly poor policy, however, in terms of careers, where the world of work is constantly changing.

The best way to acquire materials at nominal cost is by writing for them. We believe you will find a rather astounding amount available for the asking. This includes filmstrips as well as brochures and pamphlets. A second tool is preparing materials within the school. This is important in regard to cassette tapes, for example. A third tool is material from newspapers and magazines. There is so much of it—with more and more appearing in print every day. By culling such material and utilizing it, you keep your Career Education Program vital and really up-to-the-minute.

As is true in every subject area, printed material and audio-visual aids are of value. However, the value is probably less in career education than in other areas because in career education personal contacts and information derived face-to-face are far more important. Yet we certainly cannot ignore the value of articles and books, films or filmstrips. In this chapter, you will find many suggestions for obtaining or making fine materials. Because budgetary limitations are always a consideration, we will emphasize those that are obtainable at minimum cost. Furthermore, these materials are particularly good because they are current. We will, for example, recommend you have your students write for many publications. Often these are less than a year old. Books tend to remain in use for long periods of time, and, in the field of occupations, five years can make a tremendous difference. Another reason the use of pamphlets and brochures can be very valuable is that they are written by many people—often people employed in the particular field.

GUIDANCE MATERIALS

1. *The Educator's Guide to Free Guidance Materials*

The Educator's Guide to Free Guidance Materials is one of the outstanding publications in this field. Published every year by Educator's Progress Service of Randolph, Wisconsin, it is priced at less than $10. Like its relative, *The Teacher's Guide,* it contains listings of hundreds of varied materials for classroom use. Put it on your yearly requisition, because each edition has a large proportion of new offerings, so important for career education.

The Guide lists materials that may be borrowed as well as those that are sent to the school "for keeps." Films and filmstrips, for example, often fall into the first category. The printed materials do not—they usually become yours for the asking.

In 1973, the Guide listed 685 films, forty-four filmstrips, seven sets of slides, fifty-two audiotapes, five scripts, two transcriptions, one video-tape and 294 other materials—bulletins, pamphlets, charts, posters, magazines and books—a total of 1,090 selected free resource items.

There are five filmstrips (in color), five scripts, and one transcription—all free—and to be kept by the recipient.

Of these 1,090 offerings, *409* were new in the 1973 edition. New additions are starred, so that you know which you could not possibly have sent away for before without checking your catalog.

Normally about one-third or more of the titles drop out each year.

This book even contains two books in Braille or in large type for the visually handicapped.

Where do these materials come from? They come from private industry, which is alert to the changing needs of schools, and from the government.

The arrangement of the Guide is noteworthy. It has five parts:

1. Introductory information—which includes instructions for sending for material
2. Films
3. Filmstrips and Slides
4. Tapes, Scripts and Transcriptions
5. Printed Materials

Each of sections two through five is then divided into four areas:

Career Planning
Social-Personal Materials
Responsibility: To Self and to Others
Printed Materials

We suggest you have your counselors and a group of teachers study the book to determine which materials they would like to obtain, and then have a secretary send for them.

When you wish to use films, scheduling is required since, for most films, time must be allotted for the mail service.

This book can be one of the most valuable resources you own. We cannot urge you too strongly to send for it. The same is true of the book that follows, of which you should order a dozen or more copies at least.

2. *The Occupational Outlook Handbook*

The Occupational Outlook Handbook is published by the United States Department of Labor Statistics. It is a big book with nearly 900 pages of important information. It is available from the Superintendent of Documents, U.S. Government Printing Office, Washington, D.C. 20402, at the incredibly low cost of $6.25.

In the foreword of the book, Secretary of Labor Hodgson writes:

> In both human and economic terms, employment can be one of life's most rewarding experiences. A good job offers the pride of human achievement, an opportunity for individual growth and a sense of personal usefulness. It also provides the welcome security of an adequate income.
>
> But satisfied employment seldom is achieved without wise and informed career planning. Individuals must examine their own interests, abilities and goals, and must know which occupations are best suited to these traits. Future workers also must know which skills will be needed in tomorrow's working world; skills that are obsolete or in oversupply are no passport to rewarding careers.
>
> We at the Department of Labor believe that the Occupational Outlook Handbook contains information necessary to intelligent career planning. This edition provides information for more than 800 occupations so that young persons, veterans, women returning to the labor force, and others choosing careers can determine which jobs are best suited to their individual needs. The handbook discusses the nature of work in different occupations, as well as earnings, job prospects during the 1970s, and education and training requirements. This information can help tomorrow's workers prepare for jobs that have a good future in our changing society.

The handbook is published every other year. This edition, the 11th, is the 1972-73 edition. It reflects the growing demand for health and service workers, containing such careers as the biomedical engineering and electrocardiograph technician, occupational therapy aide, surgical technician, and optometric assistant. Other new careers include city managers, social welfare aides, and insurance specialists.

What makes this book so great is that it is eminently easy to read. The handbook starts with three introductory chapters designed to help counselors and students make effective use of the book and to give them a general view of the world of work. The latter is especially important for those choosing their first careers.

The main portion of the book is composed of reports on different fields of work. There are seven major divisions: professional and related occupations; managerial occupations; clerical and related occupations; sales occupations; service occupations; skilled and other manual occupations; and some major industries and their occupations.

Each career covered has the following sections: Nature of the work (which includes the actual tasks and responsibilities involved); places of employment; training, other qualifications, and advancement; employment outlook; earning and working conditions; and sources of additional information.

To give you an idea of how thorough this book is, yet how easy it is to use, here are some examples. Note they are from many different occupations.

Nature of the Work: This is from the material included on the inhalation therapist:

> Inhalation therapists treat patients with respiratory problems. This may range from giving relief to patients with chronic asthma or emphysema to giving emergency care in cases of heart failure, stroke, drowning and shock.
>
> A rapidly evolving field, inhalation therapy requires specially trained personnel to master the use of sophisticated equipment needed in treating many respiratory problems. The inhalation therapist is one of the first medical specialists called in for emergency treatment of acute respiratory conditions arising from head injuries or drug poisoning.
>
> Moreover, the short span of time during which a patient can safely cease to breathe emphasizes the highly responsible role the inhalation therapist must play. If a patient does not breathe for three to five minutes, there is little chance of recovery without brain damage, and if oxygen is cut for nine minutes he will die.
>
> Inhalation therapists follow doctor's orders in giving medication to the patient through aerosols or using mists to help control the patient's environment. When administering gases to patients, the inhalation therapist assumes complete control over the patient's environment, including moisture and temperature.
>
> Inhalation therapists may also be called upon to instruct physicians and nurses on the use of specialized inhalation equipment, and show patients and their families the proper use of home equipment. Other duties include keeping records of the cost of materials and charges to patients. Therapists are responsible for routine maintenance of their equipment.

Places of Employment: This is from the section on draftsmen.

An estimated 310,000 draftsmen were employed in 1970; almost 4 per cent were women. About 9 out of 10 draftsmen are employed in private industry. Manufacturing industries that employ large numbers are those making machinery, electrical equipment, transportation equipment and fabricated metal products. Non-manufacturing industries employing large numbers are engineering and architectural consulting firms, construction companies, and public utilities.

Over 20,000 draftsmen worked for federal, state and local governments in 1970. Of those employed by the Federal Government, the large majority worked for the Departments of the Army, Navy and Air Force. Draftsmen employed by State and local governments worked chiefly for highway and public works departments. Several thousand draftsmen were employed by colleges and universities and by nonprofit organizations.

Training, Other Qualifications, and Advancement: Note this material from the section on elevator constructors.

Although elevator constructors are highly skilled craftsmen, training is comparatively informal and is obtained through employment as a helper for a number of years. The helper-trainee must be at least 18 years of age, in good physical condition, and have a high school education or its equivalent, preferably including courses in mathematics and physics. Mechanical aptitude and an interest in machines are important assets.

To become a skilled elevator mechanic, at least two years of continuous job experience, including six months' on-the-job training at the factory of a major elevator firm, is usually necessary. During this period, the helper learns to perform all of the operations involved in the installation, maintenance, and repair of elevators, escalators, and similar equipment. The helper-trainee generally attends evening classes in vocational schools. Among the subjects studied are mathematics, physics, electrical and electronic theory, and proper safety techniques.

Elevator mechanics may advance to positions as foremen for elevator manufacturing firms. A few may establish an individually owned small contracting business; however, opportunities are limited.

Employment Outlook: Note this example taken from the section on mining.

Many thousands of new workers will be hired each year during the 1970s for exploration, drilling, and oil and gas production, to replace workers who retire, die or transfer to other fields of work.

Employment in petroleum and natural gas production during the 1970s is expected to show little change. More intensive exploration and drilling anticipated during the 1970s particularly in Alaska and off-shore, is expected to keep the number of workers at present levels despite the use of data-processing equipment and improved seismic techniques.

In addition to untrained field workers, the petroleum industry will need workers who have electrical and mechanical training or experience to maintain and repair the increasingly complex equipment.

Earnings and Working Conditions: This example is from the material on cooks and chefs.

> Limited wage data from union-management contracts covering eating and drinking places in large metropolitan areas provide an indication of earnings for cooks and chefs in 1970. In these contracts' straight-time hourly pay rates generally ranged from $2.22 to $4.65 for chefs; $2.02 to $4.12 for cooks of various types (such as pastry, fry, roast, and vegetable cooks); and $1.47 to $3.86 for assistant cooks.

At the end of each section dealing with an occupation, there is a section entitled *Sources of Additional Information.* This lists two, three or more organizations to which your students can write for further information. Furthermore, we have found that these organizations respond with an almost amazing speed; in many cases we have received the information sought within a week.

The Occupational Outlook Handbook, you will find, will be one of the basic resources your students will use constantly. It could conceivably serve as a textbook. It belongs in your media center, however, with enough copies available for your students' use.

The Occupational Outlook Quarterly, a magazine published four times a year, contains much valuable information that is "hot off the press." The Summer, 1973 issue contained such articles as:

A. "The Drive to Win: Careers in Professional Sports." Possibly any child who has hit a baseball, passed a football, dribbled a basketball, or chased a puck has dreamed of playing on a pro team. A few do, but making the big time is the toughest game in town.

B. "Manpower A.D. 2000." An excerpt from the 1973 Manpower Report of the President discusses the far-reaching effects of the nation's declining birth rate.

C. "Career Planning for High School Girls." Teenage girls must realize they are likely to work for many years and it is therefore important for them to choose a career with care.

D. "Occupational Licensing: Help or Hindrance." A new study of how and why some workers are licensed urges a number of reforms to benefit practitioner and public alike.

E. "Count on These Jobs." Whether they count logs or insurance losses, over 200,000 statistical clerks keep numerical records for business, industry and government.

F. "Outlook for This Year's College Graduates." Job offers—especially for engineers—are expected to be far more plentiful than last year. Salaries, however, will be only about 2 percent higher.

The articles, as you can see, cover a wide range of occupational areas. The cost of the magazine, by subscription, is only $1.50 per year, from the Government Printing Office.

3. The Government Printing Office

Write to have your school placed on the listing of the Government Printing Office. Each year many pamphlets and brochures are published and sent either free upon request or for a very nominal cost. They, too, have the advantage of recency, and offer a very wide variety as well.

4. B'nai Brith Vocational Service

The B'nai Brith Vocational Service, 1640 Rhode Island Avenue N.W., Washington, D.C. 20036, offers a number of publications at nominal cost which are of value in building up a resource center. Write to them requesting a listing of their publications.

5. Professional Organizations

Membership in one or more professional organizations by members of your staff is essential for many reasons—the main one being your staff can be kept in touch with what is happening in the field of career education through their publications. The American Personnel and Guidance Association is open to qualified counselors, as is the National Vocational Guidance Association, and The American School Counselor.

Membership guarantees you will be placed on the mailing list of these organizations, and along with the periodic publications, you will receive many advertisements of materials you may wish to purchase. Again, these will keep you posted on the newest material available.

The *Vocational Guidance Quarterly* has listings of career information available at relatively low cost. It also contains a bibliography of current magazine articles which are available in reprint form. (An interesting point—material is graded for vocabulary level—Advanced, Moderate or Easy. It is also rated according to N.V.G.A. guidelines.)

6. School Published Material

As your counselors, teachers, and students develop noteworthy material, duplicate it and keep it on file for future use. We have found a great deal of time may be saved when such a file is available. The results of research done by young people is very impressive to their peers. Furthermore, since the research deals with your community and can be kept up to date easily, it becomes an important tool—a really valuable part of your research center. You may wish to duplicate some of the material found in this book—such as questionnaires and curricula. These, too, may become part of your resource file.

7. Civil Service Information

The government is the nation's number one employer, employing the largest number of people in a great variety of fields. You can obtain a great amount of information by writing for it from the Federal Civil Service Commission branch in your area. This information, too, should become part of the resource center.

8. Civil Service Information in Regard to Your State and City

While not as much material is usually available in print as from the Federal Government, it is nonetheless important, for here, too, are opportunities for many of your students.

9. New York Life Insurance Company

This organization has many publications which are well worth adding to your center. Write to them for a listing at 51 Madison Avenue, New York, N.Y.

10. Publications of the Office of Education, Department of Health, Education and Welfare, Washington, D.C. 20202

The Department will send you much material in regard to career education. The bibliography contains a large number of specialized references. Other materials are being developed, which will be made available in the near future, if all goes according to plan.

11. College Catalogs

Since college will be part of the educational plan for a number of your students, it is essential that you have copies of various catalogs for them to peruse. Include both two- and four-year colleges, since both are of importance, and include every college in your area within a radius of about fifty miles. These catalogs are, of course, available for the cost of the postage required to write for them.

12. Listings of Scholarships

Send for several copies of the American Legion's book, *Need a Lift?* (The cost of fifty cents makes it a real bargain.) This, plus several of the standard references on scholarships, should be part of the resource center. It may be obtained by writing to American Legion, Washington, D.C.

13. The College Placement Annual

A very valuable resource for the high school media center is the *College Placement Annual,* published by the College Placement Council, Inc., P.O. Box 2263, Bethlehem, Pa. Available for $5, this book lists the occupational needs anticipated by 1,600 corporate and governmental employers who normally recruit college graduates. It is published on a nonprofit basis and is valuable on the high school level because it shows where the jobs actually are. (It is supplied free to college students.)

14. Newspaper and Magazine Articles

Newspaper and magazine articles collected by both the staff and the students of the Career Education Program are very important because they represent current thinking and current situations in a variety of areas. Furthermore, they are generally quite readable, which makes them of greater value to the youngsters.

15. Old Magazines

For the lower grades of the elementary school, where pictures are so important, old magazines are a fine source of photographs and sketches. Pictures of the various career clusters are essential if the different careers and occupations are to become at all real to the youngsters. Old issues of *Look* and *Life,* the various "women's magazines," *Mademoiselle,* and even *Sports Illustrated* may supply material your children will be looking for.

16. School Produced Materials

We have already mentioned printed material available from pupils', teachers', and counselors' work. We would like to suggest several other types.

A. *Tapes.* When your students interview people in various occupations, it is well worth the investment to tape-record the interviews. These can, if deemed worthwhile, be kept as part of the permanent media center. If not, it is a simple matter to retape over them.

Commercial tapes in the area of career education are available on many subjects.

If you are able to work closely with another school, you can borrow tapes and record them for your own school's use.

Tapes recording on-the-spot interviews with descriptions of the place of work in the style of radio's "You Are There" can be particularly good for "setting the scene."

B. *Video-tapes.* If your school is lucky enough to own the necessary equipment, guest speakers and interviews may be put on video-tape.

Visits to factories, stores, shipyards, or airports can be video-taped, with comments added afterward, since it is very difficult to video-tape record in a nonstationary situation.

C. *Slide or Movie Shows with Taped Commentary.* A slide or movie show can do a great deal to bring to life a work location. By adding a taped commentary, all the important data can be presented. A visit to a bank, backstage at a theater, a trip to a weather bureau or research center—all of these may be filmed with a 35 mm. or movie camera and the statistics added in pleasing form.

School-made materials of these types are more realistic than commercially produced ones because they show your community and its people in action.

In the Appendix you will find a Basic Resource Listing of Career Education Publications. These publications may be obtained at virtually no cost other than your request, and will serve to begin your library of career information.

ELECTRONIC MATERIALS

There are a number of commercially prepared career education materials that utilize electronic equipment. Some of the most specific are those produced by Xerox for the teaching of skills, such as in the automotive industry, or to prepare one for becoming a draftsman. These are discussed in detail in Chapter 12.

The Singer Company, Manpower Training Division, 3750 Monroe Avenue, Rochester, N.Y. 14603, offers career education materials as an addition to their vocational evaluation technique. Three work sampling stations are available to implement the initial system. If you're now employing this system, the new stations add approximately 300 titles to your evaluation potential. If you're contemplating the system, thirteen stations enable the use of ten basic units of career education.

CLOSED CIRCUIT TELEVISION

Much of the equipment we have just described can be utilized for large groups by the use of closed circuit television. While this will not take the place of personal visits, it is infinitely better than no experiences at all.

It is essential to prepare the students before any viewing so that they know exactly what it is they are watching for. Career education teachers should preview the material and place a list of the topics that will be discussed after the viewing on the board. The discussions will be far more fruitful as a result. Furthermore, it is more fun to watch a program after having been intellectually challenged.

COMMERCIALLY AVAILABLE MATERIAL

Write to the following organizations, explaining you wish to be put on their mailing lists:

A. Science Research Associates (SRA)
   259 East Erie Street
   Chicago, Ill. 60611

They publish a veritable library of materials, many of which can be very important tools in the Career Education Program.

Their Keys Career Preparation Program uses filmstrips and cassettes. Their motto is, "If you want to know what a job is all about, ask the person who does it." The workers were carefully chosen to represent different levels of education.

The same is true of:

B. Guidance Associates
  Pleasantville, N.Y. 10570

They put out a great many audio-visual aids which can certainly augment your program. They have, for example, "Sound Filmstrip Programs" which may serve as models for any you wish to produce, and which offer a variety of products on different grade levels.

There are many other organizations as well. We are sure you will receive mailings from them once your program goes into effect.

C. Bowmar, of Glendale, California, has an interesting multi-media program that combines sound filmstrips, cassettes, student career survey sheets, and an *Instructors' Handbook* with resource information.

"A Direction for Tomorrow" covers seven important areas. The titles are excellent: "Compassion for People" describes occupational classifications in the health service field; other areas are: "The Nation's Builders," "The Age of Electronics," "Man Has Wings," "Cabbages to Kings and Various Things," "The Money Tree," and "Jobs for the Now Generation."

Bowmar can be reached at P.O. Box 5225, Glendale, California.

HUMAN RESOURCES ARE MOST IMPORTANT: DEVELOPING A LISTING OF PARENTS AND COMMUNITY MEMBERS

The world of work is a constantly changing dynamic world—and the more your Career Education Program can foster this, the better. Extremely important ways to do this are by using speakers, panel discussions, and interviews.

It is also worthwhile to communicate with the parents of every child in the school. A simple letter and form such as the following one would suffice:

School Heading

Career Education Department

Dear Parents and Members of the Community,

We are currently developing our Career Education Program. One of the most important aspects of this Program is that it enables our youngsters to come into contact with people in a large variety of occupations. We are therefore inviting you to participate. If you care to, please complete the form below. We promise you we will not contact you more often than twice a year. If you feel this is either excessive or inadequate, please indicate the number of times more suitable for you in the space for comments. We believe you will find your visit interesting and rewarding to you as well as to the young people.

Thanks for your cooperation.

Sincerely,

_____

Head of Career Education

_____

Principal

Include a 3 x 5 or 5 x 7 index card which, after it is filled out and returned, can be filed easily.

School Heading

1. Name of child_____

   Class_____   Year_____

2. Name of parent_____ __

3. Address_____ Telephone_____

4. Occupation_____

5. Would you be willing to be considered to be a resource person in our Career Education Program? This involves being interviewed or speaking to groups of children._____

6. What time would you prefer to be reached by telephone?_____

7. How much notice would you need? One week_____Two weeks

_____or More_____

8. Would you prefer to be interviewed by the children (and the interview tape recorded) after regular working hours?

_____

9. Your comments._____

_____

10. Dates of appearance. (Please leave blank. This will be filled in whenever you join us.)_____

File the cards alphabetically under occupations, or by using the D.O.T. classification, if you prefer. However, this seems more complex than necessary. Simple alphabetical order usually is adequate.

Maintaining the speaker resource file is certainly one of the tasks of the Career Education Coordinator. It is he or she who will be in charge of filing the cards, of communicating with the parents, of thanking them after every appearance. (By letter, please. The principal should, however, sign these letters, but the C.E.C. will have actually composed them.)

Whenever a speaker comes into school, the C.E.C. should greet and personally escort the guest to wherever the children or young people will meet him or her. The atmosphere should be as pleasant, but as formal, as possible.

DON'T FORGET YOUR STAFF
WHEN COMPILING YOUR RESOURCES

Many schools have, as members of their staffs, a large number of individuals who have already had other careers, or even who are presently engaged in second occupations. Their experiences are certainly valid, and possibly even more impressive because the young people know these individuals. This includes teachers, administrators, paraprofessionals, secretaries, and custodial workers.

In one junior high school, a very quick summary revealed an engineer, a chemist, a photographer, several musicians, two profes-

sional athletes, a nurse, an actress, a laboratory technician, a legal
secretary, and an advertising executive. Such a ready-made source of
speakers can help to expand your program easily. Ask each staff
member to fill out a card with the following information:

1. Name_____

2. Previous _____ or second_____ occupation

   (check one) is_____

3. Are you aware of conditions in this career area at the present

   time?_____

4. Would you be willing to participate in Career Education Program?

5. Comments or suggestions_____

File these cards along with those received from the parents. If
you feel a need for a greater representation of careers, the C.E.C.
may write to various organizations within the community. By
enclosing the file card and requesting its return, the clerical task is
made easier. The Chamber of Commerce and Rotary and Kiwanis
Clubs are often good sources of speakers, too.

CLASS AND INDIVIDUAL TRIPS

Develop a file of class and individual trips. This may be done by
having the C.E.C. write to various organizations requesting permission for a class or individuals to visit. When the response comes back,
place the information on a file card.

After either a class or a group has visited a particular place, ask
the person in charge to list some of the highlights, and to indicate
whether the trip is very valuable, or moderately so. Many times large
groups make visits to places that are not worth the effort because the
youngsters learn very little. In this case, remove the card, or indicate
this fact on it. Sometimes, though, even a less rewarding trip is better
than nothing.

It is the C.E.C.'s task to arrange for all trips, making arrangements with the organization to be visited as well as program

arrangements within the school. He or she should arrange for transportation as well.

It is the teacher's task to prepare the young people for the trip by briefing them on what to look for. "Notice the work done by each individual," the teacher should point out. "Is there an assembly line being used?" "What chances are there for a person to use his ingenuity?" "What chance is there for advancement in this career?"

If the youngsters need specific information for any research project they are doing, they should have their questions prepared in advance.

The C.E.C. should have made arrangements for some representative of the organization to speak to the group. Without this, the visit loses much of its value. It is true the youngsters can experience the environment, and this is certainly important, but much can be added by speaking with someone who can give them specific information.

THE USE OF FILMS AND FILMSTRIPS

While films or filmstrips cannot replace actual experiences, they can add to a youngster's perceptions of the world of work. The *Educator's Guide* mentions a number that you can borrow at no cost except postage. There are many films available commercially. We cannot recommend too great an expenditure for them because they become dated, and because we feel the funds should be spent whenever possible to supply the youngsters with experiences of actual job environments and situations.

Summary

The multimedia or resource center is an important adjunct to the Career Education Program. It should serve as a place where information on a great variety of topics is readily available to the individual child. It should also serve as a repository for papers and other materials worked up by teachers and students.

The multimedia center may be as sophisticated or as simple as tastes or finances dictate. It involves collecting information, codifying it, and storing it for ease of use. This information may be part of an electronic learning system, or may use films, filmstrips, records or cassettes. It can involve pamphlets, brochures or books.

Another aspect of the resource center is the human resource one—a listing of parents, staff and community members who are willing to participate in the program by speaking, taking part in panel discussions, or by being interviewed. Still another resource is a listing of places that may be visited by individual students or by classes.

However, the most important aspect of this Program is the extent to which the pupils are involved in it. This is reflected by the young people's work which becomes part of the resource center. Research projects, films, tapes, cassettes—all made by the young people—add greatly to the appeal of the Program to their peers. Another point to keep in mind is that material must be kept current and relevant to the community in which the students live.

Like government, to paraphrase Abraham Lincoln, "Career education should be of the people, by the people and for the people."

6

Evaluating Your
Career Education Program

In the television industry they refer to the process as monitoring; in our profession we call it evaluation. By whatever name, however, systematic and ongoing examination of any program is an absolute necessity and the Career Education Program is no exception. Without this the Career Education Program or any program, can fall flat on its face. Quite often when a new curriculum is introduced with appropriate discussion and fanfare, there is enthusiasm for it on the part of the faculty—particularly if they were involved in the planning stages. (This is referred to as the "Gung-Ho" Effect.) However, unless the enthusiasm is kept up, and unless the program is constantly evaluated, it can sink quickly into ennui. Errors are bound to occur, and unless they are picked up and changed the program suffers. The best curriculum in the world on paper may result in one of the poorest in reality. Evaluation should prevent this from happening.

Who is responsible for the evaluation of the Career Education Program? The administrators, the counselors, the coordinators, and, most of all, the teachers and pupils should be consulted. In fact, everyone who is involved in the Career Education Program can and should be reached. The evaluation should always be made, however, within the framework of the total educational program of the school and the needs of the community. A Career Education Program that is totally based on college preparation, even though the large majority of students do not go on to college, is an example of the type of situation an evaluation should uncover, and which should then be quickly changed.

BASIC STEPS IN EVALUATION

In evaluating any program, there are certain basic steps.

1. First it is necessary to determine whether or not the goals that have been established are appropriate and adequate.

    a. Are the goals specific enough to give direction to the program?

    b. Are they broad enough to meet the needs of all of the children involved?

    c. Do the goals need revision? If so, what specific revision is necessary?

2. The next problem is to determine whether or not the goals are being achieved.

    a. What methods or techniques are available to objectively appraise the program?

    b. What are the subjective appraisals of it? What are the opinions of the people involved?

3. Are the methods and techniques being used efficient? Are they in need of revision?

WHO SHOULD DO THE EVALUATION?

Because the Career Education Program involves a large number of people and because of its importance to the future of each child, we suggest the principal designate a committee to evaluate the program. He or she should select some individuals who are deeply involved in it—and some who are not. (The reason for this is that those people in the former category will, hopefully, be emotionally as well as intellectually involved; they are needed because they will be able to more easily obtain information that the committee will need. The other members, those not involved, should offer objectivity.)

Let the committee (which should have about five to seven members) meet once a month to discuss developments as they occur, rather than as an afterthought. If, for example, they discover there are no trips being taken, they can take steps to remedy this situation immediately—not long after the course has been completed.

It would be part of the committee's work, too, to determine if the knowledge the pupils are getting will be of practical value to them. How often in the past have our curricula been completely divorced from the world in which our students live! Yet this cannot and should not happen with the Career Education Program.

SPECIFIC STEPS FOR THE EVALUATION OF CAREER EDUCATION

Since this program, as any educational program, begins with the efforts of the teachers, theirs should be the first reports considered.

The committee should request the teachers to fill out an analysis once in February and once again in June. The following form may be used in the elementary and junior high schools:

School Heading

Teacher _____ Class _____ Date _____

Analysis of the Career Education Program

1. What goals have you tried to reach during this period? (These may be taken directly from your syllabus.)
2. What methods or techniques have you used to try to achieve these goals?
3. Which have you found to have the most impact on your children? Which have you found to be least effective?
4. What objective appraisals have you made in this area—tests, questionnaires, biographies? What results did you obtain?
5. What is your opinion of the program? Do you feel it needs revision, and, if so, in what areas?
6. Have you found the media center adequate? If you could order more materials, what would you order?
7. What trips have your children taken? What educational results do you feel were derived? Was the trip worth the time and expense involved?
8. What speakers have your children heard? What educational results do you feel were derived?
9. How many (approximately) interviews did your children conduct?
10. How many films, filmstrips, or recordings did they use?

This survey serves two purposes. It furnishes feedback, and it also encourages teachers because it shows their work will be noted and appreciated. Far too often outstanding teaching is overlooked.

This will not happen if the evaluation form suggested is used. The conscientious teacher's reports will stand out clearly from any others.

TEACHER EVALUATION IN THE HIGH SCHOOL

If there is a ninth grade in your high school, it would be involved in the Career Awareness part of the program, and, as such, the teachers would use the preceding form.

For the tenth, eleventh, and twelfth grades, the following form would be more suitable:

School Heading

1. Teacher_____Class_____Date_____
2. Course being given_____
3. To which career cluster is this related?
4. What are the jobs for which this course prepares students?
5. What specific skills are taught?
6. What specific "tools of the trade" have the students learned to use? How much practice have they had in using them?
7. List the students who have been placed in jobs based on their work in this course. Separate full-time, part-time or cooperative education programs.
8. How might the course be improved? What equipment or other supplies would be needed?
9. How have the students been made aware of the actual job situation? (Visits, speakers, films, etc.)
10. How have the students been made aware of the following:
     a. Job opportunities in this field
     b. Chances for advancement
     c. Jobs in related areas

After the forms have been filled out, they should be submitted to the committee for review. Of course, other aspects will be considered such as the following pupil evaluation.

PUPIL EVALUATION

It is essential for the teacher to learn whether or not the material he or she is teaching is getting across to the children. This is always done, in part, by teacher observation, particularly in the lower grades.

In the first grade, the teacher's evaluation will be mainly subjective in nature, and consist of anecdotal records or comments made by the youngsters.

In the second grade, the evaluation will still be subjective, but the teacher should look for clues throughout the school year that indicate the children are forming positive attitudes toward work and towards themselves in relation to the world of work.

The children may be asked to do the following:

1. Make a list at the beginning of the school year, and then again at the end, of all of the occupations they know. A comparison of the lists is one indication of some of the material the child has absorbed.

2. Ask the children to list the five things they learned which impressed them most.

From the third grade through the ninth, as the Career Education Program proceeds, at the end of five and then of ten months, questionnaires should be given to the students to determine the following:

1. The extent to which they have learned about the world of work. This would be reflected by a knowledge of factual material.

2. The extent to which their attitudes reflect an understanding of various concepts which were studied, such as the connection between entry-level jobs and skill training.

3. The extent to which they are able to relate career education to their own lives as evidenced by their plans for the future in terms of career choice and the training for it.

4. The extent to which they are aware of career needs within their own communities and within the nation.

5. The extent to which they are able to relate their school work to their future educational needs.

Of course, in the lower grades questionnaires are not as reflective of the children's achievements as they are in the junior high school. However, they do offer the pupil a chance to pull his or her thoughts together, and to try to focus on the entire term or year's work.

Because each class and each teacher will cover different material, it is essential that the teacher develop his or her own questionnaire. (By making this a questionnaire, and not a test, better results will be obtained. And there are certainly no yes-or-no answers.)

At the end of the questionnaire, each child should be given the opportunity to make suggestions for the improvement of the Career Education Program.

In the high school, students in skills courses should be asked to evaluate their experiences in much the same way as the teachers.

1. What course is being taken?
2. What career cluster is this related to?
3. What are the jobs for which you feel this course will prepare you?
4. What specific skills are you learning?
5. What "tools-of-the-trade" have you learned to use?
6. What actual job experiences have you had?
7. How have you learned about actual job situations?
8. What have you learned about the job opportunities in the field?
9. What have you learned about chances for advancement?
10. What have you learned about jobs in related areas?
11. How could this course be improved?
12. What other courses would you like to see offered?

Every student above second grade should be asked to fill in an evaluation questionnaire which is given to his or her teacher, who will study it and submit it to the committee for further review.

EVALUATION BY OTHER MEMBERS OF THE STAFF

Any program will have a greater chance of success if it is fostered and nurtured by the principal. If he or she visits the classrooms, talks to pupils and parents as well as teachers, and is involved in it, the program will probably thrive. These visits and conversations also help the principal to evaluate the program. If the classes do not appear to be vital, the principal can usually see this in a very few minutes.

Supervisory visits by other staff members often are quite effective. They, too, serve to inspire teachers—because the teachers realize they may be observed. You may wish to send notes to your teachers asking when they would like to be observed as they are teaching career education. It is good practice to visit the classrooms and to have informal as well as formal observations on record. It is also important for supervisors to be well-versed in the curriculum and in the actual performance of it, because invariably many questions are asked by parents, by members of the community, and by members of the school board. Having the answers at one's finger tips can be a tremendous asset. This is especially true of career education because of the large amount of information put out by the Federal government in recent years. The news media have given career education much time and space, and the general public is becoming quite aware of the need for it. We would venture to say it is second only to reading in terms of the publicity it has received.

Funding is another reason the supervisors should have the facts at their finger tips. The Career Education Program requires funds for new printed materials, for audio-visual aids, and for trips in the elementary and junior high schools. In the senior high it requires many new courses be instituted, which, of course, necessitate the employment of teachers—many of whom are specialists in their fields. The principal and his supervisory staff should be able to discuss all of these expenditures in terms of their value to the students.

THE CAREER EDUCATION COORDINATOR

The Career Education Coordinator should certainly report to the committee on the progress of the program. He or she will be able to correlate the factual information, possibly using the form that follows:

Statistical Survey of Career Education Program

Date_____

Number of students on register:

Number of students involved in program:

Number of student hours spent in program:

Number of teachers teaching program:

Number of other staff members (administrators, paraprofessionals, etc.):

Number of trips taken:

Number of speakers presented:

Number of interviews:

Number of films and filmstrips shown:

Number of films and filmstrips available:

Number of books and pamphlets available:

Number of cassettes and tape recordings used.

Number of cassettes and tape recordings available:

Number of pupil-prepared materials produced:

Is there a teacher training program? Length of time spent on it:

Are there Teacher-CEC-Administrator conferences? Number and length of time spent on them:

Suggested improvements:

Funds needed:

This form, combined with the evaluations done by pupils, teachers, parents, and community members, will form the basis of the study by the committee.

PARENT EVALUATION

You may wish to involve parents and community members in your evaluation—if not after every five months, then after each year. For the Career Awareness part of the program this may be done by questionnaires, by interviews, by conferences, or by workshops.

1. Questionnaires

Do not use very long, involved questionnaires. For example, the following should prove adequate:

To all parents:

a. Are you aware of the work of the Career Education Program in your youngster's class? How did you learn about it?

b. Do you feel your child is learning about the world of work? On what do you base your answer? Please give examples.

c. Do you feel your child is getting experiences which are educational in regard to occupations? Please give examples.

d. How do you feel the Career Education Program can be improved? Please give specific suggestions, if possible.

2. Interviews, Conferences, and Workshops

In all of these situations, parents will be talking with teachers or administrators. This enables them to discuss the Career Education Program. Much the same material should be covered as is listed above, with suggestions and comments written down as they are verbalized.

Suggestions from parents can often be very valuable in terms of improving the program. Furthermore, this may bring offers of assistance.

EMPLOYER EVALUATION

Employers of high school students should certainly be consulted in regard to the training they are receiving in the skills courses. As graduates of skills courses are employed, the employer or his representative is in the position to judge how adequate the training offered by the school was:

Has the student been prepared to perform all of the tasks required by the job?

Can he or she handle the tools required?

Does the young person show a comprehension of the principles underlying the work?

Is he or she willing to do an appropriate share of the work which must be done?

The employer is also able to judge the attitudes of the graduate toward his job and toward his fellow workers:

Is he or she punctual?

Is his or her attendance good?

Is he or she cooperative?

Is he or she pleasant?

All of these aspects of working, and many more, should be taught both in Career Awareness and in the skills courses as part of the Career Education Program.

Employers can evaluate the skills courses being offered in terms of their needs, which are, of course, representative of a fraction of the needs of the community. In some areas, where one or two industries hire a great many people, cooperation with the personnel departments of these industries is essential.

Employers should be interviewed by the C.E.C. or by a member of the Evaluation Committee, since their opinions must directly influence the skills courses, both as far as selection and content are concerned.

In the cooperative education programs where actual job experiences are provided while students are in school, evaluation goes on constantly. Students are paid employees who spend part of the school day at work, part attending classes. Cooperative education programs are planned, organized, and supervised by teacher-coordinators working with school personnel, parents, students, and employers. Planned on-the-job experience and coordinated in-school instruction are the essential elements that make cooperative education programs different from part-time employment for general work experience. An advisory committee and a training plan for each student are significant features of the cooperative education plan. Evaluation is built into the program—and is done constantly. An employer (or his representative) evaluates the work being done by the student and after a period of time, if his or her work is unsatisfactory, the student is dropped from the program.

REVIEWING THE RESULTS AND EVALUATING YOUR PROGRAM

After all of the evaluation materials are gathered and studied, the committee should determine whether or not the goals of your Career Education Program are specific enough to give it adequate direction. However, it must be remembered these are the goals for an entire Career Education Program ranging from grades one through twelve. Individual schools will not have adopted all twenty of these goals. Those that your school is using are the ones to be considered.

The goals are as follows:

1. To help each youngster develop an awareness of himself and of his place in the world of work.

2. To develop an awareness of the huge variety of careers possible.

3. To develop an awareness of what specific tasks each career actually entails.

4. To develop an awareness of the career ladder concept and of the various levels of careers, depending on the education or training required.

5. To make every academic subject more meaningful and relevant through the use of the basic concepts of career education.

6. To develop an awareness of the connection between academic achievement in the elementary school, its continuation in high school, and its further continuation in college.

7. To make education meaningful to all of the students—those planning to terminate their education immediately after high school, or who plan to attend college, technical, or vocational school afterward.

8. To understand the economic facts of life and their connection with education or training.

9. To develop an awareness of the need for the young woman as well as the young man to learn skills and to prepare for a future career.

10. To develop an awareness of the time and money required for a person to be trained or educated for a specific career.

11. To develop an awareness of the availability of funds to every student for furthering his education.

12. To develop the concept of career by choice, not chance, and to develop techniques for doing full career studies.

13. To develop methods for the young people to examine their personalities and attempt to find careers that will bring them job satisfaction.

14. To offer specific vocational or technical training to those who plan to terminate their education after high school.

15. To offer academic preparation including advance placement courses to those preparing to enter college.

16. To develop an awareness of the availability of training and education at any time in the individual's life—enabling him to obtain new skills, and therefore to make himself more valuable to his employer.

17. To develop an awareness of what is expected of a person "on-the-job."

18. To understand the role of the guidance counselor in assisting the individual in his assessment of his talents, abilities, and personality in terms of career choice and subsequent success.

19. To develop an awareness of the preparation for, and precautions involved in, going into business for oneself.

20. To involve the entire faculty, the parents, and the members of the community and, above all, the students, in the Career Education Program.

Summary

Your Career Education Program should be evaluated constantly if it is to be as successful as possible.

In evaluating it, the goals should be considered first: Are they adequate? Are they being achieved?

Evaluations should be done by teachers and administrators, by students, and possibly by parents and community members. On the high school level, if pupils are employed outside of the school, their employers' opinions must certainly be taken into consideration. All evaluation should be done in writing, and forms have been included in this chapter for that purpose. These forms should then be reviewed by a committee, working with the principal. Any changes or improvements shown to be necessary should be done as quickly as possible; hopefully there will be some so that the program will grow and develop.

PART TWO

The Curriculum

This section of *Administrator's Guide to a Practical Career Education Program* includes a full curriculum beginning with grades one and two, and going up to the high school. It may be used exactly as it is given, or it may be changed to suit the needs of your community.

In passing this curriculum on to your teachers, please make the following points:

1. It is essential that they know what specific material the youngsters have studied in previous years.

2. If the career education program is being introduced, and taught for the first time, each unit (going back to the first grade) should be covered—of course at the youngsters' level of comprehension. Some of the concepts are not repeated, and yet they should be included in every child's education.

3. Every unit may be enlarged upon, and, indeed, should be—if it stimulates the children's interests.

4. Activities have been included for each unit, but these are given to serve as a beginning. Their number should be increased as class participation dictates.

5. Since the career clusters are referred to throughout these pages, they are included, with a listing of appropriate careers within them in the appendix.

6. We have suggested that the teacher permit the youngsters to decide upon the careers they would like to study. They should not be permitted to restudy units they have recently covered. They should be helped to choose careers which are to be found in abundance in your area of the country. "Lumbering" may be interesting but hardly of practical value in Boston. If, however, it is decided to cover it in Boston, less time should be spent on it than on a unit in automobile servicing, for example.

For additional information about careers, your teachers should be supplied with copies of the *Occupational Outlook Handbook*. There should be copies of the *Dictionary of Occupational Titles* in the library. Both of these references are published by the Bureau of Labor Statistics, of the Department of Labor.

7

Career Education
for Grades One and Two

In the primary grades we are interested in approaching Career Education from two directions. One is to help the youngster develop career awareness. The other is to help him develop self-awareness. Then, as the child matures, this knowledge is combined so that he is able to place himself realistically in the world of work.

Many young children have ambitions. "When I grow up I want to be a fireman," Billy says. "I want to be a nurse," Mary Ann announces. But these proclamations are based on the fantasies of childhood. As the youngster grows and is educated, we hope to have him or her develop goals that stem from his or her own talents, aptitudes, likes, and dislikes; and which also stem from a knowledge of what, specifically, the career of his or her choice entails.

This introductory phase of the Career Education Program aims to:

1. Arouse the child's curiosity in regard to the working world.
2. Encourage wholesome attitudes toward all types of work.
3. Enlarge the child's occupational horizons.
4. Answer the child's many questions concerning occupations.
5. Introduce and begin developing basic concepts through meaningful activities.[1]

The following attitudes and concepts are the basis for the work of the first and second grades. Accompanying each are activities to help develop them.

---

[1] Teacher Resource Guide K-617 Career Awareness & Attitude Development, State Dept. of Education, Cheyenne, Wyoming p. 17

I. SELF-AWARENESS

Unit A. There is a dignity in all work people do.

Have children define word "dignity." You may bring in the word "respect." Do all people have dignity? Are all people worthy of respect?

1. What work do people you know do? Draw pictures of people at work.

2. What work do the adults in your family do? (Avoid use of "father" in the question. There are many homes where there is no father. If the children bring up their fathers' occupations, there is no problem; but maintain the questioning without being specific.) Include the work done in the home, as well as outside.

Make a huge bulletin board display showing pictures of people at work. These may be drawings or photos cut from old magazines. (Note to teacher: Have children bring magazines in for this purpose. Also collect them yourself. They are an excellent source of material. The same is true of the magazine section of newspapers.) Label the display "The World of Work."

3. What work is done in your home?

Have the children list the various tasks done in their homes. Find pictures, or draw them. Include them in "The World of Work."

4. What work do you do? Help the children to realize they have tasks to do at home which are work. However, their main work is in school. Add photos of the children at work. (Have them bring them in or take Polaroid photos.) Develop this concept at length. Children's place of work is school. Their actual duties are the activities on which the class works.

5. Discuss how each member of a community helps the others by working in or out of the house. Have children illustrate or act out the roles of each person.

Unit B. Every boy or girl will be able to choose a career for which he or she will have to prepare.

Define "career" as the skills people learn to fit them for a special place in the world of work. The teacher can point out, "I cannot be an engineer. I can't do any of the things an engineer can do. Why not?" List many careers. Have children tell you why you can't function in them. Then ask, "But why can I be a teacher?"

Define "job" as a place where a person can use the skills he has learned, and get paid for the work he does.

Discuss such places—businesses, institutions, and opportunities for self-employment. Have children list careers that may be found in each of those areas. They may act out some of these careers (charades), or play "20 questions." The children can guess either the career or the place where the person is employed.

Unit C. It is important to find a career one enjoys. Some people have careers they like. Others do not enjoy their work.

1. Have children interview people they know, asking "What do you do when you work? Do you like your work? Why or why not?"

2. Discuss the results in class.

3. Make a graph showing the number of people who enjoy their work, and those who don't. Include a category in between as well.

4. Find or draw pictures of people who appear to be enjoying their work. Include photos of children in school.

II. CONCEPTS

Unit D. What things do people need in order to live?

1. Food, shelter, clothing, are the basic essentials. Then include education, transportation, light, heat. You may wish to include fresh air, a nonpolluted environment, and pure food (without adulterants). Discuss what is included in each of these categories: Food—including beverages, sweets, etc. Shelter—include home furnishings. Clothing—stress the fact we all have changes of clothing, that our clothes must be kept clean and in good repair.

2. All of these necessities imply jobs that must be performed to supply them.

Unit E. Where do people get the things they need?

Role-play sources—farmer, milkman, food market operator, clothing store salesperson, etc.

Stress the part money plays in every transaction.

Discuss the barter system: "If you and your friend each wanted something the other person had, what could you do?" Can you do this in stores? Why or why not?

Use newspaper advertisements to show the prices of various items including food, shelter, clothing.

Where do *you* get the things *you* need?

Have each child make a drawing or montage showing the things he or she needs. Discuss each piece of work to see if anything has been omitted.

Unit F. What does the expression "earning a living" mean?

1. Clarify the idiom "making money."

Who is permitted to "make money"? Where is it made? Are you allowed to even draw a dollar bill? What happens to counterfeiters? Do a bulletin board display of man in jail for making money. Label it "People Who Try to Make Money Spend Time in Jail Instead."

2. What is the difference between "making money" and "earning money"?

How do people in various parts of the world earn their livings?

Discuss farming countries such as India where many people work just to supply the food their families need.

Why don't children have to "earn a living"? Years ago they did. If you wish you may discuss child labor in this country, as well as abroad. Stress that today children's work is in school, so they may prepare for careers as adults.

Unit G. What do people you know do to earn their livings?

Ask the children how they can learn about the careers and jobs their friends and relatives have. Go over the specific questions they should ask. For example, "What do you do when you work?" and "Where do you do your work?" Have the youngsters report back. Try to obtain as much variety as possible.

Keep a huge chart of "The World of Work" with pictures of people in these career areas.

If the children wish to invite speakers to talk with their classmates, or if you wish to invite their parents or friends to speak, we suggest you tape record the talks. They may be used with the children later in the term or with other classes. (Again, avoid the stress on parents, particularly in an area where there are many broken homes.)

In this unit, have children list as many occupations as they can think of, with a brief description of each. Do this as an experience chart; that is, have the youngsters suggest the careers while you write them down. Then duplicate the material in booklet form for the class to use. Including small cartoons adds to the fun. Have the class do the designs, and select several to illustrate the careers. If you have talented artists in the class, include explicit pictures.

Unit H. Why should girls as well as boys prepare to earn a living?

1. How many women do you know who work outside their homes?

Ask children to make a list of the different careers they have.

2. Years ago women had to do all the work of providing food and clothing for the family. Now they have many machines to help them.

What are some ways modern science has helped the homemaker? Have children bring in pictures of labor-saving devices.

3. What are some careers women have been working in for many years?

"Look around you," tell the children. "What careers do you see in your school?"

Then go into hospital work, office work, entertainment.

Have children role-play some of these careers.

4. What are some careers that have recently become available to women?

Newspapers carry stories of more and more women entering careers previously thought of as men's. These are often in science, construction, and communication.

Watch for these articles and use them as the basis for discussion and for a bulletin board.

5. Why do women work?

Ask children if they know families where the woman must support the family. Discuss possible causes such as accidental death of the husband or divorce.

Bring out idea that with labor-saving devices women have more time and want to work. Also, some women want to contribute money to the family income.

Invite a female member of the school faculty to discuss her career with the children.

Unit I. How can you learn about yourself so that you can prepare for a career?

1. Have two students stand in front of the room. Ask the rest of the students to tell you in whole sentences how these two students

are alike and how they are different. This may be repeated with several pairs of students. The teacher can explain that we are alike in some ways and different in some ways and it is good to know as much as we can about ourselves.

2. Place pictures around the room of children engaged in various activities—playing, sleeping, eating, running, etc. Let each child select which activity he likes to do and tell the class why he likes this activity. Point out that because each of us is different in some ways from everybody else we like to do different things.

3. Make individual books over a period of time of drawings with captions on different pages such as the following:

   a. Things I play with
   b. My family
   c. Things I can do
   d. Things I like
   e. Things I'm afraid of
   f. Things I can't do now
   g. I would like to be . . .
   h. I would not like to be . . .
   i. Things that make me laugh
   j. Things that make me cry

(This activity may run throughout the year. It need not be limited to one particular time.) Encourage children to express their own ideas in their pictures (and short stories as well, if writing activity is feasible to include here.)

Unit J. How will the subjects you study in school help you towards a career?

A. Why do you need to know how to speak well?

Question the children. How many jobs can they think of in which it is necessary for a person to be able to speak well? Bring in their experiences watching television (lawyer, policeman, salesperson) and their experiences in school. Then discuss people they meet in their neighborhoods (storekeepers, doctor, nurse, clergyman).

What happens if a person doesn't learn to speak well? (He cannot make himself understood, and then he would have difficulty dealing with people in any job.)

What do people do who are not able to speak in a normal fashion? (Elicit the idea they created a language in which they use hand signals to convey their ideas.)

How can you help yourself to learn to speak well? (Bring out the idea that when young people hear good speech, they can imitate it.) When they get the opportunity to speak in class, they should. Point out this is one aspect of education which will help them in everything they do—socially as well as vocationally.

B. Why do you have to learn to read in order to have a career? (Ask the children to try to think of some careers where they *never* have to read.) This is difficult, since most careers involve filling out an application for a job, and if a person can't read it, he cannot fill it out. Secondly, there is the matter of being given instructions in writing. Most of the time there are some instructions it is necessary to read.

Set up a role-playing situation in which someone has to be able to read instructions and cannot do this. What happens if he just forgets to do so?

Discuss the fact that for many, many careers it is necessary to get training either in high school or in a college or technical school after high school. If a person doesn't read well, he will have difficulty all the way along the line.

Set up role-playing situations showing how reading is important to

1. a truck driver making deliveries
2. a waitress
3. an actress
4. a salesperson
5. a secretary
6. a doctor
7. a carpenter
8. an automobile mechanic (who has to read the manuals put out by automobile manufacturers)
9. a housewife

Why else do people read?

1. For pleasure
2. To learn things they cannot learn any other way.
3. To keep up with what is going on in the world.

C. Why is it important for a person to be able to do arithmetic in terms of his future career and life?

Again, try to find a career where there is no need to do some arithmetic at some time.

Then have the children list careers that are based on arithmetic—bank tellers, bookkeeping, selling, carpentry.

Show how a housewife must know arithmetic to avoid being cheated when she shops.

Why do you need to be able to do arithmetic when you buy something?

Unit K. Why is it important that you finish jobs that you start?

1. Discuss with children:

   What things have I started but never finished?

   What was the result of this?

   Why would it have been better if I had finished?

2. You may wish to rexograph a picture that is completed by connecting numbers. This illustrates the need for completion.

3. In order to produce a product, a person must finish the tasks assigned to him. Give the children some task to do—something which will yield a product when finished, but which is not worthwhile unless completed. It might be a picture to color, a booklet to make, a decoration to construct—but whatever it is, it must be an item which is not worthwhile unless completed.

4. Have children role-play jobs that are obviously harmed by a person not completing what he started. For instance, a carpenter not completing a house he starts work on, a nurse not giving a patient medicine, an automobile mechanic not tightening the screws after he changes a tire, or a sewing maching operator not completing a garment. Have children point out the results.

Other concepts you might include in your program, if you have the time for them:

1. Develop the awareness that many pieces of work consist of a number of steps, all of which must be completed for the piece of work to be done.

2. Develop the awareness that a person must be able to follow instructions in order to successfully finish his work.

3. Develop the idea that not everyone is good at the same things other individuals are good at. Some people have certain talents, others have different ones. It is important that we discover our talents.

4. Develop the idea that some people are good at physical work, some at mental work, some at both. We have to learn what our strong points are and make use of them.

5. Develop the idea that people are constantly faced with the need to make choices, and that a person must learn to make decisions.

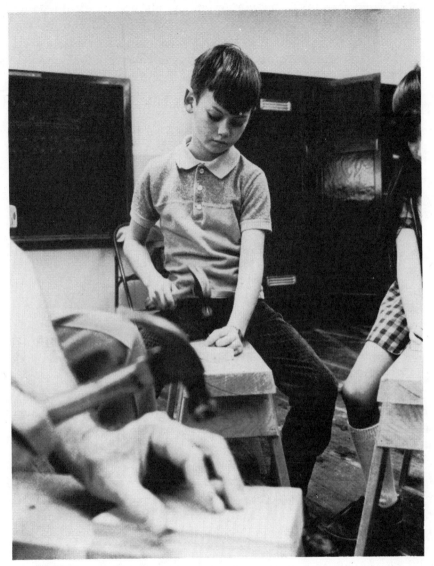

WSCOE

CAREER AWARENESS

The following units are based on specific career areas. These are derived from the career clusters outlined by the Office of Education, Department of Health, Education and Welfare. Introduce the concept of career clusters to the youngsters. A cluster consists of a group of related careers (see Appendix B). Many people decide on the career cluster they want to enter and then select a specific career. Others choose a career without considering any other.

In teaching any cluster, introduce it and ask the children to name as many careers in that cluster or area as they can think of. Then allow them to select the ones they wish to study. You may then invite a speaker to discuss the career; or you may show films or a filmstrip. Even very young children can look at books and, as the children mature, they may read books on the subject. In these grades, the study of a career should include the duties involved (what a person actually does) the personality qualifications, and the training a person would need to pursue that career.

The cluster is covered by the title of the unit which follows:

Unit L. Which workers produce our food? (This cluster is "agri-business and natural resources.")

Let us assume the career selected for study is the dairy farmer.

Unit M. How do people in business or office careers help us (business and office cluster)? This unit is given in detail to serve as a model.

Because of our involved way of life. (We don't grow our food—we buy it. We don't build our own homes, or supply our own light, etc.) Therefore, we need businesses to help supply us with the things we require.

Have class list all careers in business.

Let us consider *bookkeeping:*

What are the bookkeeper's duties? The bookkeeper keeps records of what people buy, and how much they pay for each item. If they do not pay the whole amount, the bookkeeper keeps a record of how much is owed.

The bookkeeper also prepares a list (called a statement) usually once a month to show how much money has been received by the business.

The bookkeeper is also in charge of paying bills. When anyone in a business buys something, the bill is sent to the bookkeeper for payment.

Sometimes bookkeepers write all of these numbers by hand. Often they use machines.

Some large businesses have more than one bookkeeper. If they have a number, there is usually a head bookkeeper to tell each one what to do.

What are the special things about bookkeeping for a person to consider? A bookkeeper should be a person who enjoys working with numbers. He or she should enjoy working very carefully, and should be someone who wants to work in an office. Most bookkeepers work by themselves, rather than with other people. Bookkeepers have to be able to stay in one place for long periods of time.

Where can a bookkeeper prepare for his or her career? Most bookkeepers (nine out of ten) are women who learned their skills in high school or junior college. Almost all have graduated from high school.

Activities

Invite a parent who is or was a bookkeeper to speak to the class, describing his or her job, and showing the children how books are kept. (Request the person keep this simple, so that the children are not overwhelmed.)

Have the children do simple transactions and enter them "in books."

Have the children make a list of places where bookkeepers work.

Draw a "tree" of people who work in offices.

Unit N. How do people working for the telephone industry help us? (Cluster is communication and media)

Why is the telephone important to most people? Have children role-play a telephone conversation. Then discuss careers in this industry. Ask, "Who put the telephones into our house? Let's talk about the telephone installer."

Unit O. Who builds the houses people live in? (The construction cluster)

Elicit from the children the workers they can think of who are involved in building houses. Ask what each worker does and draw a house to represent the construction industry.

Have the children fill in bricks with the various careers of people who take part in the building.

Have the children list some of the tools used by these workers.

Do any of these workers wear special clothing? Why?

Have the class choose one career for investigation.

Unit P. Who plans our meals in school so that we get the foods that are best for us? (This is the consumer and homemaking education cluster.)

Elicit from the children the fact that too much candy is not good for them. They will probably be able to tell you why. Then go into a discussion of a balanced diet, by asking, "If you could plan your own meals, what would you eat?" Ask this question of many of the children, writing some of their replies on the board. Then question them to determine whether they are aware of meal planning. Introduce the idea that one person is responsible for meal planning in the school. This is the dietician.

The remaining career clusters and suggested careers for study in the first and second grades are as follows:

Units Q-Z.

Environment—forester or geologist
Fine arts and humanities—actor, artist
Health—medical technician or nurse's aide
Hospitality and recreation—playground supervisor or tennis teacher
Manufacturing—power tool operator or inspector
Marine scientist—marine biologist or marine geologist
Marketing and distribution—salesperson or buyer
Personal services—barber or dry cleaner
Public service—teacher or fireman
Transportation—pilot or stewardess.

Of course these would be studied on the children's level of comprehension. Please note, though, that we have tried to include careers on every level—from semiskilled through professional.

The number of careers to which you introduce the children may be as many or as few as you feel the children can handle. However, even at these grade levels, do not cover them superficially. Include the detail we have suggested.

8

Career Education for Grades Three and Four

This chapter, the previous one, and the one that follows are divided into two major areas—development of self-awareness and of career awareness.

Since this is a continuation of the Career Education Program begun in grades one and two, we will assume the children have already become familiar with certain aspects of the world of work covered in Chapter 7 and we shall build on those. Should it be necessary to teach them or reteach them, please do so—since those learnings are basic to the concepts that follow.

In grades three and four we seek to:

1. Expand the child's awareness of the vast number of careers available to him.

2. Investigate a number of specific career areas in greater detail, including duties, personal qualifications, and education or training necessary.

3. Take into consideration the child's talents, abilities and hobbies, and encourage him or her to think about utilizing these as possible bases for career choice.

4. Consider the various levels of employment and relate them to educational training.

THE CAREER EDUCATION NOTEBOOK

Have each child set aside a portion of his looseleaf book (or an individual notebook) for career education material.

After each unit, have a short summary written and placed in the notebook. (You may prefer to rexograph and distribute the summary.) However, there should be some means of recording material.

Reiterate the important facts. While there should not be quizzes or formal tests in this subject area, review material should be available and gone over from time to time for reinforcement.

Photographs, drawings, and commercially prepared material from magazines, pamphlets or newspapers may be collected and added to the notebook. This often serves as an incentive and is another way of reinforcing what the child has learned about careers.

Unit A. The kind of work a person does affects his entire life.

1. The teacher may ask the children how many of them have ever moved and why they moved. Of those who moved the teacher may ask how many moved because of their fathers' occupations. Discuss how work frequently determines where people live.

2. The children may dramatize the following situation with possible solutions:

Mr. and Mrs. Black have three children. Mr. Black is an electrician. He puts electric wires in new houses. No more new houses are being built in Greenwood. What can Mr. Black do?

3. A committee of several children within the class can be appointed to interview a moving van company to find out how many families they move every week and how far the families usually move. Have the committee report back to the class.

Unit B. Learning to cooperate is very important in school as well as later on, in the world of work.

1. Have children role-play a family scene in which everyone is going his own way. Assume a meal is in preparation. What might happen without cooperation? Do the same in the classroom. Be sure to bring out the fact that it is often difficult to accomplish what one sets out to do without the cooperation of others.

2. Have the children list careers in which cooperation is a must, and those where it may not be quite so necessary.

3. Do a mural of the class working together titled "Class XY Works Together." Have everyone make some contribution to it.

4. Have each child interview a worker he or she knows, asking, "In what ways do people cooperate with you when you work? Is this cooperation important?" Have them report back to class.

5. Have children collect pictures for their notebooks showing people working well together.

Unit C. To pick a career wisely, a person has to understand himself or herself.

1. You may use a checklist as a means of helping your youngsters to learn about themselves.

Checklist—"Say Hello to Yourself"

1. Do I like to be outdoors?	Yes____	No____
Would I like to work outdoors in the winter as well as in the summer?	Yes____	No____
2. Do I like to be with other people?	Yes____	No____
3. Would I rather have a job alone?	Yes____	No____
4. Do I like to help other people?	Yes____	No____
5. Do I like to use machines?	Yes____	No____
6. Do I like to sell?	Yes____	No____
7. Do I like to work with my hands?	Yes____	No____
8. Do I like to work in an office?	Yes____	No____
9. Do I like to work with animals?	Yes____	No____
10. Can I take orders from other people?	Yes____	No____
11. Would I like to help people who are sick?	Yes____	No____
12. Do I like to sew?	Yes____	No____
13. Do I like to read and do library work?	Yes____	No____
14. Do I like to build things?	Yes____	No____

Have children discuss their responses. Point out the purpose of this is to help each child to understand himself or herself a little bit better. Have each child place this in his or her Career Education notebook.

2. Have the children ask someone they know who is employed to answer the questions in the checklist, and then to see if their career choice took these aspects of personality into consideration.

3. Ask each child to write some words about the person he admires most. Then ask, "Would you like to be that person? Why or why not?"

4. Have children think of as many different careers as they can for Billy and Bobby Bonn.

Billy Bonn is a strong young man who is rather shy. He likes to work outdoors and he enjoys hard physical work.

Bobby Bonn is Billy's brother. Bobby loves to be around people. He is always talking to others, and he always seems to be having a good time.

Have them draw Billy and Bobby each sitting under his own

tree. Put the names of the various careers on the leaves of the trees under which Billy and Bobby Bonn are sitting.

Unit D. Hobbies and interests sometimes lead to careers.

1. Have children talk about their hobbies and interests. Then ask, "If you wanted to use this hobby or interest as the basis for a career, what would it be? Why?"

2. Ask the children if they possibly can, to think of someone who used his or her hobby or interest as the basis for a career. Ask them to tell their classmates about it.

3. Have the children list and illustrate those hobbies that might lead to careers.

4. If possible, invite persons whose hobbies or interests became careers to speak to the class about them. Such people might include a photographer, the owner of a pet shop, or a person in a stamp and coin collecting business.) Be sure, however, to point out to the children that choosing a career based on a hobby or interest is only one way of basing an occupational choice—and it is an unusual person who finds his career this way.

5. Many famous inventors had careers which were based on early interests and hobbies. Have the children read about Thomas A. Edison or George Washington Carver, for example.

Unit E. There are a great many careers in the area of science and/or health.

1. Have children bring in pictures of people whose careers are associated with science or health. Make a large montage of these.

2. Have them check for newspaper and magazine articles about such careers.

3. Divide the class into committees. Have each committee study one career in the field of engineering—these include civil, chemical, aeronautical, sanitary, electronic, mechanical, and electrical. Have them report back to the class showing how the engineer in every branch of engineering works to improve our lives. (This activity is best for bright children.)

4. Take the class on a trip to a hospital that has facilities for tours. If none is available, take them to the office of a doctor or dentist, or to a medical laboratory. Discuss with the children, before they go on the trip, exactly what it is they are looking for.

In the hospital have them list the different jobs they see people performing; if they have the opportunity to ask questions, have them speak to these people to get more information.

5. Have the class visit the library, and see how many books they can find which are related to science or health careers. Assign a different book to as many children as possible and have them report back to the class, telling them what they have read.

Unit F. There are many careers that are concerned with entertainment or recreation for others.

1. Have children determine how many hours a day they work. How many do their parents? How do they spend their leisure time? How do their parents spend their leisure time?

Show the number of careers which are involved in giving others enjoyment.

2. What are the "fine arts"? Have children list these and the careers associated with them. Many people involved in these careers have become quite famous. Point out a number of artists in all of the fine arts areas.

3. In what way would professional athletes fit into this career area? Have children make several montages—one of people in the arts, the other of athletes.

4. Discuss fine arts and professional sports as a means of earning a living, pointing out the need for another career, if a person does not have the talent and good fortune to become successful in either of these areas. Refer to this as a "back-up" career.

5. Invite a person whose career is in one of these areas to speak to the class. Ask him or her to include specifically how he or she was able to succeed (because of much practice, hard work, great perseverance, and often doing without money for some time).

Unit G. We need both producers of services and producers of goods.

1. What are services? Have children list all the careers they can think of which are involved with services. These include personal services and public services, as well.

2. Divide the class into buzz groups. Have each work on a play showing what would happen if only one particular service area disappeared. Cover a lack of barbers, policemen, television repair men, sanitation men, dry cleaners. Encourage the children to make their plays humorous but factual.

3. Have children bring in or draw pictures of people at work producing goods. They may do research to learn about the vast numbers who were involved in producing the rockets that went to

the moon, for example. Then show how many are involved in the production of a man's suit.

4. If possible, arrange for a visit to a local industry. Make arrangements, too, for some person to take the class on a tour to explain to them what each of the workers is doing.

5. If this type of tour is not available, use a film that shows some type of manufacturing.

6. The children may create mobiles depicting the need for various workers in the community. The teacher may stress the need for a "balance" of producers of goods and services in making the mobiles.[1]

Unit H. In order to be able to fill a job, a person must have certain skills.

1. Ask children, "Why can't you be an airplane pilot—right now?"

Develop the concept that a pilot needs to know exactly how to do many things, such as using instruments and taking off and landing a plane. All of these are skills.

Next develop the idea that the mechanic who checks the plane before take-off also needs skills. Then continue with other airline personnel, such as the stewardesses, the baggage handlers, and the reservation clerks.

Compare the number of skills the pilot has with those of the reservation clerk.

2. Have the children interview people they know, asking them, "What skills do you have that enable you to do your job? Where did you learn those skills?"

Try to assign as many different careers as possible. Include members of the school staff—teachers, librarian, secretary, custodian, fireman (if there is one).

When children report back, have them list their findings. You may want to duplicate the list and distribute it.

3. Develop the concept of a career and a job. Where else, besides in a school, could a teacher use his or her skills? What are some careers or jobs listed in the help-wanted columns? Have the class bring in a newspaper showing some of them.

4. Discuss which skills a person learns in elementary school. Why are these important?

Divide the class into committees. Have each committee list a

[1]Wyoming, p. 95.

series of careers that use reading, writing, spelling, arithmetic, and scientific knowledge.

Of course, there will be overlapping since some careers may use every subject area mentioned.

Unit I. There are many skills involved in working on any job. You learn a number of them in school.

Set up a make-believe or an actual business of some sort with your class, and structure the class so they actually conduct it.

a. A grocery store selling candy and snacks. Have the children purchase goods, calculate costs, mark-ups, etc.

b. A grocery store using empty cans and boxes from real products. Encourage the children to bring in as many of these as possible from a large variety of products. This will give the class an opportunity to study prices as well.

For products such as meats or poultry, use simulated packages, but be sure to include these very important items.

Have different children act as cashiers, checkers, and stock boys. Give each one the opportunity to "make change." If you can beg, borrow or steal an old cash register, this will add much fun to the lesson.

c. A toy store, in which they may sell their old toys (in good condition) or ones they construct.

d. Have them create small sculptures or greeting cards, clothes-pin dolls, Easter eggs or Christmas decorations. You can have them make "play money" to use to purchase these things.

You may have the class raise plants and run a plant sale. The best time for this is just before Mother's Day. Start with seedlings; if you wish them to start with seeds, begin much earlier in the year.

Make the situation as businesslike as possible.

Point out the differences between producing a product and purchasing it.

Unit J. People learn the skills they need for their careers in many different places.

Some skills are learned on the job. Others are learned in high school.

1. Have the children list careers which they think could be learned on-the-job.

2. Select ads from the help-wanted section of the newspaper; have the children pick out those which offer on-the-job training.

3. Have a discussion to bring out which worker would be worth more money to an employer—one who has skills or one who has to be trained on the job. (Do not, however, encourage the children to look down on any type of employment.)

4. What skills can be learned in the high schools in your community? Have children check this with older brothers and sisters. Send a committee to speak to the principals or guidance counselors of local high schools to obtain this information and report it back to the class.

Unit K. People also learn skills in special schools and in colleges.

1. Have the children check the local telephone directory for the name of any schools in the area. Find out what courses they offer by telephoning or writing to them.

2. What two-year colleges are in your community or neighboring ones? For what careers do they prepare people? Take the class on a visit to the college. Visit the library and several of the buildings, if possible. Choose a time when the campus is not too crowded.

Ask a representative of the college to speak to the boys and girls, discussing the careers for which they might prepare at that college. Obtain copies of the college catalog.

3. What four-year colleges can be visited by the children? (Follow procedures just outlined.)

4. Which careers can pupils study in two-or four-year colleges?

Make a bulletin board display. Cut oaktag into the shape of huge buildings. Label one "two year college prepares for careers in . . . ." Label the other "Graduating from four years of college prepares a person for a career as a . . . ." If you prefer, have a montage of people engaged in these careers posted on the oaktag.

Unit L. The more education and skills a person has, the more money he usually (but not always) earns.

1. Have children look at the help-wanted ads for this. Make a list of occupations on different skill levels, and compare the salaries offered. Cut out some of the advertisements, and paste them on a large chart.

Point out there are far fewer professional jobs than there are semiskilled, and the children will have more difficulty finding them in the ads.

2. Have pupils imagine they have to decide right now whether they will be going to college or not. Have them discuss the pros and

cons. (Pros—better salary, more interesting work, meet more people. Cons—requires two to four years of college, sometimes even more, fewer positions available, more responsibility.) You may wish to do this in buzz groups.

3. Discuss professional sports or the entertainment field. Ask pupils to read a biography of a famous athlete or entertainer (or read excerpts to them). Point out how long it usually takes to get that "big break."

Introduce the concept of a back-up career—of preparing for something else so that if the entertainment or sports career doesn't work out, the person has something to fall back on. (Carroll O'Connor of Archie Bunker fame was a junior high school teacher before he became successful in television. The same is true of Sam Levenson, who taught in high school.)

4. Have pupils interview their families or others they know, asking, "Why is it important for a person to have some skills to offer to an employer?" Then discuss the responses they received with the entire class.

5. Have children draw graphs of the following statistics:

The income listed is an estimate of all the money a person earns from age 18 until he or she retires:

If a person has less than eight years of education (if he doesn't graduate from elementary school), he will probably earn $213,505.

If he graduates from elementary school, he will earn $276,755.

If he has from one to three years of high school, he will probably earn $308,305.

If he graduates from high school, $371,094.

If he has from one to three years of college $424,280.

If he graduates from college $584,062.

If he goes to college for advanced work, $636,119.

These figures are based on the figures supplied by the Bureau of the Census, 1970.

Unit M. There are different levels of employment, depending on the skills a person has learned. Unskilled jobs require physical labor, semiskilled people have some skills. Skilled workers have learned a number of related skills. Technical careers involve many skills, and professional jobs even more.

1. Put the five career levels—unskilled, semiskilled, skilled, technical, and professional—on the board. Have the children list occupations in each group. Then have them bring in or draw pictures of people engaged in these areas of work.

You may vary this by placing the titles of various occupations on index cards (use 5 x 7 size). Then place the career levels on the top of large sheets of construction paper. Have the children attach the cards to the charts. Retain these charts for future use.

2. Review meanings of the levels of employment. Bring out the concept that unskilled labor may be very hard work, because if a person has no skills he must offer strength instead.

Semiskilled workers usually operate machines of one kind or another. This requires a few skills.

Skilled workers know a number of skills.

Technicians are skilled in doing involved tasks, usually using technical equipment. They are trained in what to do and how to do it.

Professionals have been trained for long periods of time. They are usually given a problem or a piece of work and have to figure out how to solve or accomplish it. Often they give instructions to the technicians or the semiskilled people.

3. Have the children write a class newspaper, including stories about people on all occupational levels and what duties their careers involve. Show which skills they need. Include a variety from each skill level.

4. Invite a speaker from your State Employment Service to discuss white-collar and blue-collar occupations. Then you may have the children make two life-size figures, one covered with blue denim, the other with an old white sheet. Have each child paste a label on either figure, with the name of a career printed on it.

Unit N. Where a person lives determines many of the careers open to him.

1. Use the filmstrip "Where People Live and Work" put out by the Visual Educational Consultants. Have children look for the following information:

What occupations were shown?

What geographical areas?

What effect does geographical location have on occupation?

2. Divide the class into buzz groups. Ask each group:

    a. To think of as many occupations as they can which are found in other sections of the country, but not in theirs, (Cowboys and lumberjacks are examples.)

    b. Then have them list those which are found in their areas, but not in others.

    c. Next ask them to figure out, from looking at the help-wanted section of the newspaper from your community and several nearby, which occupations are in greatest demand.

Discuss the findings.

3. Obtain want ads from several small and large communities. Have children read these, and again determine in which occupational areas there are the largest number of jobs.

4. If there is a parent or community member who has worked in a number of geographical areas of the United States, ask him to address the class, telling them how his work was similar and how it differed in various parts of the nation.

5. The children may read about a variety of occupations. For example:

Burt, Olive. *Peter's Sugar Farm,* Holt, 1954.

Brooks, Anita. *The Picture Book of Fisheries,* Day, 1961.

Colby, Carroll. *Park Ranger,* Coward, 1956.

Lent, Henry. *Submariner,* Macmillan, 1962.

Hyde, Wayne. *What Does a Diver Do?* Dodd, 1961.

Sterling, Dorothy. *Wall Street,* Doubleday, 1955.

Munzer, Martha, *Unusual Careers,* Knopf, 1962.

THE CAREER CLUSTERS

In the units that follow five more careers will be outlined, based on the career clusters. These are to serve as models.

For each cluster, teach the vocabulary necessary for the children to understand the unit fully.

Please plan to cover careers from every one of the clusters. Listings will be found in the Appendix.

On the third and fourth grade level, go into more detail in terms of exactly which tasks the person performs in a particular career.

As you begin each cluster, ask the children to list as many careers in that unit as they can. Then have them select the ones they wish to study. You may have the class divide up into committees, or work as a committee of the whole.

Do not allow the children to repeat work they have done in previous classes unless they are vitally interested in a particular career; if this is true, then be sure they add to their knowledge of it—and don't waste their time. It is better to select related careers and have them work on these than to redo material they have covered before.

Unit O. Fine Arts and Humanities.

Introduction: Men and women engaged in occupations in these career areas give other people enjoyment.

Ask children what their families do during their waking hours when they are not working. Develop a series of activities. Then link careers with these activities, for example, "My father plays golf."

What careers can you think of related to golf—golf 'professional,' caddy, groundkeeper.

"We watch television. . . . "

In listing the careers associated with television, include backstage personnel as well as the entertainers themselves. In this chapter, the career of the broadcast technician is examined in detail.

The Broadcast Technician

Duties. The broadcast technician sets up the electronic equipment that is used to record or transmit radio and television programs. He or she works with microphones, sound recorders, lighting and sound effects devices, television cameras, tape recorders, and motion picture projectors. He or she must be able to operate all of this equipment and keep it working properly.

A broadcast technician may work in the control room regulating the quality of sounds and pictures being recorded or broadcast, or may operate controls that switch broadcasts from one camera or studio to another, from film to live programming, or from network to local programs. By means of hand signals and, in television, by use of telephone headsets, he or she gives technical directions to personnel in the studio. When working on disk jockey programs, he or she sometimes operates phonograph record turntables. Other control room duties may include operating movie projectors, making recordings of live shows, and keeping an operation log of all broadcasts.

Special Qualities. A young person interested in becoming a broadcast technician should plan to get a Radiotelephone First Class Operator License from the FCC. Federal law requires that anyone who operates or adjusts broadcast transmitters in television and radio stations must hold such a license. Some stations require all their broadcast technicians, including those who do not operate transmitters, to have this license.

Young people must work hard to find jobs in the broadcasting career area.

Education and Training. To become a broadcast technician, the person may go to a technical school or college after high school. Being a "ham radio" operator is also good training. So is working on a high school or college radio station.

Many schools give courses to prepare the student for the FCC license test.

Activities. Try to arrange for a trip to a broadcasting studio to see the technician in action backstage.

Invite a person who works in this field to speak to the youngsters to discuss this career and others related to it.

Simulate a broadcasting studio, with children making the props and creating equipment from cardboard, etc.

Write up in experience chart form the activities of the broadcast technician.

Have the children discuss the role of the technician in terms of the programs the children view. For example, if a program is taped or video-taped, what does this mean? If it is "live," what does this mean?

Unit P. The health careers.

There are a great many careers to be found in this area. Furthermore, the field is a growing one, with modern technology causing new needs for more personnel.

As a sample of the careers in this cluster, we have chosen *the pharmacist*. (The children may refer to him as the druggist, although that title is disappearing.)

Unit Q. The hospitality and recreation cluster.

Americans have much more leisure time now than we have ever had before. It's expected we'll have even more in the future. Discuss what people do during their leisure time and vacations. Many people travel. There are a number of careers connected with traveling. Have the children name some.

For career study, consider the hotel manager.

Unit R. The manufacturing cluster.

Almost 20 million people were employed in manufacturing in 1970, nearly 5.5 million of them women.

In manufacturing there are careers on every level—professional, technical, skilled and semiskilled. However, only 10 percent are in the professional category, while most are skilled or semiskilled.

For our example of a career from this cluster, we have selected the *sewing machine operator.*

Unit S. The marine science cluster.

Although man has been aware of the riches of the ocean for many, many years, it is only now that they are being seriously considered as sources of many things we need. In the career areas in marine science these, plus other factors, are considered. For career study we have selected oceanography.

9

Career Education for Grades Five and Six

Before covering the material in this chapter, it is essential that you cover the information in previous chapters. They contain basic concepts the child must comprehend if he is to develop an understanding of the world of work and of his place in it. Rather than list them again, we are relying on your use of both Chapters 7 and 8 for this essential background information. It may not be necessary to teach each unit; you must be the judge of this. The children's sophistication must certainly be considered, but it cannot be taken for granted. Assume your children know very little about careers, and proceed from there.

THE PERSONAL ATTITUDES OF THE TEACHER

In teaching Units A through I, as the first activity begin each unit by asking the following questions:

1. What skills do you learn in this subject area?
2. What talents do you need?
3. What personality traits would be useful to a person majoring in a career related to this subject?
4. What career areas are related to this subject area? Have the children name as many as possible. Then have them select those on which they wish to concentrate.

Unit A. What are the careers associated with language arts?

[Writer of books (fiction and nonfiction); Writer for magazines (fiction and nonfiction); Writer for newspapers—Reporter, Analyst, Editorial Writer; Writer of plays and scripts for movies, television, theatre; Actor; Director; Lawyer; Poet; Advertising; Teacher (all grade levels); Editor (books or magazines); Radio and Television Announcing; Directing and Performing; Business—Secretary, File Clerk, Receptionist]

Activities

1. Have class write to the editor of a local newspaper, requesting a tour of the plant and a discussion of careers in journalism.

2. Assign one career to every two children. Have them work up a script role-playing that career.

3. Develop a class Career Book to which each child contributes. Make this a unit of work with drawings, photographs, newspaper articles, and reports by the class done in the same manner as described in the previous chapters.

Establish a staff with editors and writers to publish the book. When it is completed, duplicate and distribute it to every child in the class.

Unit B. What careers are based on arithmetic or mathematics?

[Accountants, Architects, Engineers, Bookkeepers, Cashiers, Surveyors, Draftsmen, Mathematicians, FBI Agents (Accountants), Consumer Researchers, Computer Programmers, Bank Tellers, Stock Brokers, Internal Revenue Agents, Tax Specialists, Salesmen, Businessmen, Teachers]

Activities

1. Have the class secretary write to the FBI asking if a speaker could be sent to discuss FBI careers with the class. Have children prepare a list of questions to ask him.

2. If there is a computer installation in a convenient location, arrange for a visit and request one of the programmers to discuss his work with the children.

3. Teach the children how to function as cashiers. Have them make change. You may wish to train them in the correct writing and handling of checks and traveler's checks as well as cash.

4. Teach several of the elements of bookkeeping. Give the children a series of figures to enter and keep. Make these interesting by showing profit and loss.

5. Introduce the concept of income tax and filing forms to the class. Have them do the calculations on the simple forms.

6. Allow the children to play Monopoly and other games that

illustrate various principles connected with arithmetic and mathematics.

Unit C. What careers are connected with science?

[Chemist, Orderly, Physician, Nurse's Aide, Dentist, Practical Nurse, Veterinarian, Registered Nurse, Meteorologist, Medical Laboratory Technician, Oceanographer, Medical Laboratory Technologist, Dental Assistant, Dental Hygienist, Physicist, Engineer, Pollution Controller, Teacher of Sciences]

Activities

1. Divide class into buzz groups. Discuss the following:
   a. Why do people enter the health professions?
   b. What personality traits should they have?
   c. What are some of the advantages of a career in this area?
   d. What are some of the disadvantages?
   e. What are some scientific careers not directly associated with health?
2. Which jobs could be considered entry-level jobs? Skilled? Technical? Professional?
3. Have class bring in photographs and make a large montage of science careers. Do a second one of just health careers.
4. Arrange for any parents who are involved in either health or science careers to discuss their work with the class. Have children prepare questions beforehand. Request the speaker to show the children one of the skills he or she uses (e.g., taking pulse). Also request the person to discuss the skills he or she has had to learn for use in this career area.
5. Have children write to the Peace Corps (Washington, D.C.) asking for information in regard to careers in it which use science to help mankind.

Unit D. What are the careers associated with social studies?

[Social Worker, Historian, Psychologist, Economist, Teacher, Journalist, Recreation Specialist, Drug Addiction Service Worker, City Planner, Lawyer, Politician, Travel Agent, Job Interviewer, Anthropologist]

Activities

1. Have entire class read a newspaper or magazine. Each select one story that shows the writer's knowledge of history.

2. Ask for representative of the local Department of Social Services to send a representative to discuss the Department's careers with the class.

3. Hold a "brainstorming" session to show how effectively a group of people may work together. For instance, ask each child to write down the first thing that pops into his head when you say "cooperation." Compare the responses and list them. Show how this type of thinking can be used in a class and in a business situation.

4. Invite a lawyer to address the group, discussing how he or she was educated to enter his profession, the examination which had to be passed, and the actual work—on a day-to-day basis.

5. Visit a playground with the class. Ask the playground director to discuss his or her career, why he or she entered it, what skills he or she needs and uses.

Unit E. What careers can people with talents in art or music consider?

[Art: Illustrator; Commercial Artist; Cartoonist; Greeting Card Designer; Art Teacher; Designer—fabrics, clothing, furniture; Decorator, Sculptor, Photographer

Music: Musician—popular or classical; Singer—popular or classical; Music Teacher; Composer—popular or classical; Instrument Maker, Instrument Repairer]

Activities:

1. Invite the music and art teachers to discuss careers in their respective fields. Ask them to include the concept of talent being necessary to succeed in these fields, and the art teacher to show examples of his or her work. (The music teacher may also do so.)

2. Have children compile a series of materials showing illustrations, advertisements, cartoons, and greeting cards.

3. Ask the class to read a biography of a famous artist or musician. Discuss these in class, bringing out the amount of training and experience needed before success is reached. Point out that some artists never are commercially successful in their lifetimes.

4. Have children select and carry out one of the following activities:

    a. Prepare drawings for advertising copy for a specific product—to be used in a newspaper advertisement.

    b. Do a cartoon.

    c. Design a dress, car, piece of furniture, or fabric design.

d. Write advertising copy using photographs cut from magazines.

e. Make a montage or collage showing a variety of musical instruments.

f. Make a design on a linoleum block, and using this make several designs (rows, alternates, etc.) for gift wrapping paper.

Unit F. There are careers associated with health education and sports. What are they?

Professional Sports   Resort Personnel
Playground Director   Physical Therapist
Coach   Dancer
Teacher of Health Education Recreation Director in play-
in Regular Schools   grounds, day care centers

Activities

1. Invite a professional sports person to speak to the group, discussing how much practice is involved before a person can qualify for professional sports. Ask this person to mention the need for a back-up career.

2. Have the children do research among the people they know to determine:

a. How many have careers related to sports?

b. How many have hobbies related to sports?

c. Make a graph with the results submitted by the entire class, showing the results. You can break the results down into the various sport areas.

3. Discuss the concept, "The importance of leisure time and physical education activities." Reasons:

a. More time—35-hour week, 4-day week. (People used to work 60 hours a week; then 40 hours; now often 35 hours and decreasing.)

b. Today there is more awareness of the need for physical activity for maintaining good health.

4. Have class name as many careers related to this area as possible.

a. Salesman of sports equipment

b. Gardeners who maintain golf courses

c. Life guards

d. Swimming pool builders

5. Discuss with class which careers can serve as a part-time source of income (while one is in college, for example). Lifeguard, golf caddy, and skating rink attendant are some examples.

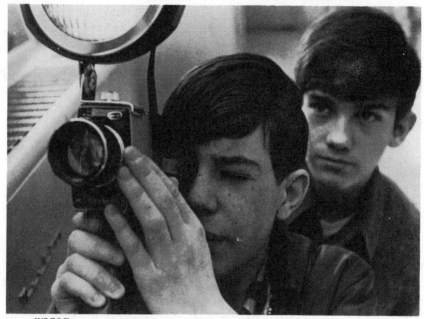

WSCOE

Unit G. In junior high, senior high, and college you may be studying a foreign language. What are the careers this might lead to?

[Interpreter, Teacher, Salesperson, Business Executive dealing with firms who do business with other countries, Importer, Journalist (assigned to a foreign country), Government Worker, Dubber of foreign language films]

Activities

1. Have committees write to the U.S. Government and to the Departments of the Army, the Navy, and the Marines, asking what careers are available to young people speaking foreign languages. Ask specifically for women as well as men.

2. Have children purchase copies of foreign language newspapers and display these in class. If possible, ask for parents or friends to translate some of the headlines or articles.

3. Tune in to a foreign language program on radio or TV.

4. Discuss and, if it is at all possible, visit the United Nations and see the simultaneous translation being done by the interpreters.

5. Take class to see a foreign language film. PREVIEW IT YOURSELF FIRST! Choose one that is on their level of comprehension and suitable for them.

Unit H. What careers will you be able to select from if you find you are interested in industrial arts?

[Carpenter, Cabinet Maker, Plumber, Electrician, Stone Mason, Glazier, Floor Layer, Tile Setter, Roofer, Tool and Die Maker, Printer, Photoengraver, Operating Engineer (heavy equipment), Custodial Engineer]

Activities

1. Invite an industrial arts teacher from junior high school to discuss courses and careers with the class. If the children have never had any shop experience, try to arrange a trip to the junior high school for them. Ask that at the time the teacher relate the visit to career orientation.

2. Take class on a visit to a construction site. Arrange for the builder or foreman to discuss various career areas available.

3. Invite parents and community members who are involved in any skilled craft to speak to children, describing their work in terms of duties, advantages, and chance for advancement. When possible, request them to bring their tools and show their use.

4. Draw a large diagram showing a house under construction with men working on different aspects of home-building. Have children label each career area shown. Include as many as possible in the diagram.

Unit I. What careers involving home economics (do not restrict this cluster to girls) are there for us to think about?

[Cook, Chef, Restaurant Manager, Dietician, Registered Nurse, Practical Nurse, Interior Decorator, Clothing Designer, Tailor, Couturier, Consumer Tester, Journalist]

Activities

1. Arrange for a behind-the-scenes visit to a large restaurant. Instruct the children that they may ask questions they have planned in advance.

2. Have children point out the practical value of home economics in terms of their present and future lives.

3. Have the class interview the school dietician. Ask her to describe the various careers involved in preparation of food for the students. (If there is no dietician, invite one from another school or from a local hospital.)

4. Have students collect pictures and materials from magazines and newspapers relating to careers in home economics and make a montage. Include articles that show the work of people in the home economics area.

Unit J. Many more careers are not directly related to any one subject area. They use the knowledge you have learned in not one but most of your subject areas. What are some of them?

Activities

1. Have class list as many areas as they can which are not directly related to school subjects.

Business	Sales
Clerical	Forestry
Automotive	Fishing
Printing	Mining
Manufacturing	

2. Manufacturing industries of all kinds supply careers for many Americans:

    a. What are some of the things Americans manufacture in factories?

    b. What are some of the things made by hand?

    c. What kinds of careers are there in factories in your area?

    d. Have class make a magazine showing the variety of products manufactured in factories.

3. Arrange for a visit to any factory in your community. Request the personnel manager to show the boys and girls the various careers to be found there.

4. Visit a port and have children learn how materials are brought into and leave our country. Discuss careers involved, such as customs inspectors, stevedores, seamen, etc.

How has "containerization" affected shipping? How has this affected career opportunities?

5. Invite a high school guidance counselor to speak to the class in regard to careers they can prepare for while they are in high school. These would include clerical and business subjects in the academic high schools and a variety of subjects in the vocational schools. If the high schools are comprehensive, explain this.

Unit K. Are you interested in working for the government?

There is a large variety of careers available through working for the government—federal, state or city. These range from semiskilled through professional and managerial. Many of them, but not all, require the person applying to take an examination. If they pass, their names are put on a list from which they are appointed. The government is the largest employer in the United States.

Activities

1. Have the class secretary:

   a. Write to the U.S. Government Printing Office, Washington, D.C., for a list of career areas within civil service.
   b. Designate several committees to write to both your state and city governments for listings of job areas.

2. Invite the principal of the school to discuss opportunities within the school system—not only for teachers, but for paraprofessionals, aides, librarians, psychologists, and counselors. List the requirements for becoming a teacher and the benefits of getting additional training beyond the B.A. degree.

3. Take the class on a trip to the local police or fire department. Ask for a person to discuss career areas with the youngsters.

Point out that there are some fire departments which are volunteer, meaning there are no paid careers within them, since the members donate their services.

4. Ask the children in which city they would expect the most career opportunities to exist in work for the Federal government. Draw a diagram of the Capitol and other government buildings, and on it have the children write in the names of various career areas to be found there. Don't forget to include the various elected and appointed officials who, after all, also work for the government. These would include the President and others in the executive branch, members of the Supreme Court and others in the judicial branch, and the members of Congress in the legislative branch.

Unit L. Are you interested in working for yourself?

Many people prefer to be in business for themselves. They may start a business, purchase an established one, or enter a family business. This business may sell services (such as a dry cleaning store) or products (a grocery). What kinds of businesses are there in your community?

Activities

1. Have class draw a large chart showing the community and indicating the businesses or factories on it. Indicate what each one is, and approximately how many people are employed in each.

2. Have children prepare another large map; check the local newspaper for advertisements; cut them out and paste them on the map.

3. Arrange for class committees to interview some of the local business people. Work out questions beforehand. Have children suggest what they would like to find out as they do this interviewing. For example:

   a. When did you go into business?

   b. How did you start this business?

   c. How many people do you employ?

Be careful to have them avoid any questions that might prove embarrassing.

4. Have children add to the map of businesses the vacant stores in the community. Check these to find out what types of establishment they were before they closed. Discuss the possible reasons for their having closed.

5. Have children interview people they know who are in business, asking what they feel are the factors necessary to succeed. Discuss the findings, and make a class listing of them.

Unit M. Why is it very important to be happy in one's work?

We give the name job satisfaction to this concept. (Be sure children understand the word "satisfaction" since it is so basic to the concept.)

Activities

1. Have children calculate the number of hours they spend "working" in school. Have them compare this with the number of hours people usually work.

Have them compare the number of years they will be in school if they graduate from high school and from college. Compare this with the number they may expect to work in their lifetimes.

Have them calculate, too, the number of leisure hours they will have—so that they see the comparison between work and leisure. Have a chart drawn to show this.

2. Have each child interview one person to find out how he feels about his career:

    a. What things does he like about it?

    b. What things doesn't he like?

    c. Would he choose it again if he could, or would he choose some other career?

Discuss the findings, tabulate them, and have the children draw conclusions. (Be sure women are interviewed as well as men.)

From the data obtained above, have the class draw conclusions.

3. Have each child describe the career he thinks would bring him job satisfaction including, of course, his reasons for selecting it. Tell the children beforehand that these paragraphs will be read aloud. When they have completed them, do so, without mentioning names. Have the children guess which of their classmates wrote which paragraph.

Have class judge whether the reasons are valid, and tabulate them.

4. Have committee make a bulletin board of photographs of people who have said their jobs bring them job satisfaction, with their reasons listed below. Invite one or several of them to speak to the class.

Unit N. Preparation for your life's work.

All of your years in elementary school are preparation for your career. All of your years in high school and in college are too. In what ways do they prepare you?

Activities

1. Have the children list the number of direct connections they can see between schooling and careers. For example, in order to be a lawyer, a person must be able to read and to study the law. A secretary must be able to spell well. A parent must be able to help in the education of his or her child.

2. For each career area you will cover in the career clusters, teach the vocabulary involved with the career.

Have the children design their own greeting cards and keep a log of their work in school. Select activities that are career oriented as you teach subject matter.

3. Allow children interested in becoming teachers to teach. Work with them beforehand, helping them to prepare the lessons.

Arrange to have your "student teachers" teach other classes, especially kindergarten, if you can obtain the necessary cooperation of the other teachers.

4. Set up tutoring within the class for those pupils who need help by those competent to do it.

5. Set up a "student court" and have the children role-play to show how a lawyer functions. Do the same type of role-playing for any area where it is applicable—acting and directing, ball playing and coaching, for example.

Unit O. What happens when people are replaced by machines?

Activities

1. Discuss concept of technological unemployment in terms of careers that virtually no longer exist in our country—such as the tinker or the lamplighter. Have children name any they can think of.

2. Discuss those careers that are less likely to be needed than they used to be. Include industrial and manufacturing jobs.

3. Next, cover careers that are relatively new—from the last half of this century. These would include work on computers (electronic data processing), and on aerospace experiments of all kinds.

Have children make charts illustrating all of these concepts.

4. Arrange for a trip to a railroad yard (which is now largely automated), or to a computer installation. Many hospitals and police stations, or the state office of the United States Employment Service, may have a computer which they would be willing to demonstrate.

5. Have children ask their parents and grandparents which careers they can recall that no longer exist.

Unit P. Why do you think it better for a person to choose his career rather than go into it by chance?

1. When one chooses one's career, he or she is able to select one which will be enjoyed, and one which uses his or her talents.

2. A person who selects a career will learn the skills he needs and be prepared to take his place in the world of work.

Activities

1. Divide class into buzz groups, and have each discuss the following topics:

a. Is it silly for a boy or girl in this grade to select a career? Why, or why not?
b. Why is it easier to change a career selection while a person is still in school?
c. Could a person change his career after he has begun working? Why is it more difficult then?
d. How can young people be helped to think realistically about careers?

Have each buzz group report its findings back to the class and discuss the results.

2. Have children list several career choices and retain these papers. Next have them read the want ads to see if there is any demand for these careers. Point out, however, that not all career openings are listed. A great many are not.

3. Have pupils again interview friends and relatives to find those who actually chose their careers and those who drifted into them. Discuss their findings. Have them work on two charts comparing the two groups. (Make sure they ask *why* people chose their particular careers.)

4. Discuss the so-called glamour careers, and the need to choose a back-up career so that, in the event the first career is unattainable, there is the second to fall back on.

Often teaching is chosen as the back-up career, although selling, waiting on tables, or even driving a taxi are examples of other back-up careers which have been chosen.

After covering these units, go into the career clusters in greater depth. You are able to use the materials in the two previous chapters for the first eleven career clusters. The remaining four follow.

THE CAREER CLUSTERS

In the fifth and sixth grade, try to introduce careers with which the children have had little personal contact, as well as those they see on a day-to-day basis.

Unit Q. Marketing and distribution.

This career cluster is composed of careers with which many of your students are familiar. These include workers and managers in retail stores, plus wholesalers or distributors. After a product is manufactured it must be marketed or sold. We shall consider the role of the buyer in a department store, rather than the salesperson because a career as a buyer is one with which your children are probably unfamiliar.

THE BUYER

Duties

The buyer in a department store has the responsibility of purchasing goods for a special department. He or she must select the merchandise and be able to calculate approximately how many items of a particular type the department will be able to sell. The better it sells, the more successful the buyer is.

If the buyer makes purchases unwisely, the merchandise may have to be sold at a lowered price or returned to the firm from which it was bought.

The buyer keeps track of the stock that has been purchased. He or she determines the price, basing this on the wholesale price plus the amount the store must add to this in order to cover expenses and make a profit. When the goods must be marked down, the buyer calculates exactly how much, and when to do so. The buyer works with the sales department in regard to selling the merchandise.

When a buyer selects new merchandise, he or she looks at the variety available from different manufacturers. Buyers must be aware of style changes and trends in clothing, home furnishings, and other items. They must select items which customers will find attractive and which they will purchase.

Often the buyer introduces the new merchandise to the staff— particularly the selling personnel.

Special Qualifications

Buyers must know their customers and be able to purchase merchandise that will sell. They must be aware of prices from different manufacturers, and be able to select the merchandise offering the best sales potential and the best value. They should be energetic people who can share their enthusiasm with others.

The buyer must have self-confidence and be able to deal with manufacturers. He or she must be able to work well with others since his career involves dealing with sales people, customers, manufacturers, and supervisors.

Buyers may have to travel and may be required to work evenings and other irregular hours to prepare for sales and holidays.

Education and Training

Some buyers work their way up from other positions within the organization. However, a bachelor's degree, with a major in marketing, is becoming a necessity. There are also special schools that train people for careers in retailing.

Useful college courses include business administration, marketing, retailing, buying, and economics. However, liberal arts students, engineers, home economists, and other graduates have been successful in the field of buying.

If one is interested in a career in this field, it is a very good idea to work during the summer in a retail store to experience the environment and get a taste of what the work is like.

Activities

1. Arrange for a trip to a large department store, with a tour "back stage" if possible. Request the personnel manager to speak to the group, describing the careers to be pursued in a department store.

2. Have students role-play applying for a job in a department store. Have them analyze some of the careers available in terms of personality traits, and in terms of which personality traits would make a person unsuitable for such a career.

3. What other sales careers are available? Have class check help-wanted columns to learn where the job opportunities are in the area in which they live.

4. What knowledge would a salesperson need? Discuss concepts of knowing the produce one sells. For example, a person sells plants, he or she should be able to give instructions for the care of the most frequently sold plants at least.

5. Have class discuss the work of the buyer, then imagine themselves to be toy buyers, and write compositions describing the toys they would buy for their departments for Christmas, taking into account the different age groups of the children for whom they were buying.

Unit R. Personal service.

In this career cluster are barbers, cosmetologists (hair stylists, hair dressers, manicurists), waiters and waitresses, bartenders, guards and watchmen, and people involved in such industries as dry cleaning, laundering, and shoe repairing. We suggest you study the cosmetologist for this cluster.

Unit S. Public service.

The career we have chosen to represent this career cluster is a familiar one to the students. Yet, in spite of this familiarity, there is probably much they do not know about being a police officer. Go into these careers in detail.

Unit T. Transportation.

The transportation cluster includes careers in aviation—such as pilots and copilots, flight engineers, stewards and stewardesses, aircraft mechanics, airline dispatchers, air traffic controllers, ground radio operators and teletypists, and traffic clerks and agents. In the field of the merchant marine, there are careers as officers or unlicensed merchant seamen. In railroading, there is a variety of careers, such as locomotive engineers, locomotive firemen, conductors, brakemen, telegraphers, station agents, clerks, signal workers, track workers, and bridge and building workers. Another industry in the transportation cluster which is extremely important is that of trucking, with many people employed in this area. Study the pilot in depth.

10

Career Education for Grades Seven, Eight, and Nine

In this chapter we shall suggest several approaches to Career Education for use with grades seven, eight, and nine. The first is based on the plan as outlined by the Office of Education. The alternatives are other interpretations that may prove to be more practical, depending on your particular school system. It is essential that your program be based on the needs of your students and your community, and that it be set up with these needs foremost in mind. We see absolutely no point to preparing youngsters for nonexistent jobs. While it is worthwhile to introduce as many career areas as possible, it seems ridiculous to go into in-depth training when, at the end of that training, the young adult will become frustrated because there is no place to utilize the training for economic gain. As you plan your program, give this concept first priority. The Assistant Secretary of Education, Dr. Marland, stated in a speech to the Pennsylvania Personnel and Guidance Association: "The program (career education), if it is to be built, will be built by people like you across the land. We in OE (Office of Education) will encourage, provide money and technical assistance, but no approved solutions." If we are to build programs that will be of value, they have to be tailor-made to our own particular situations.

THE OFFICE OF EDUCATION APPROACH

The OE has made certain recommendations and suggestions. In regard to the junior high school grades, it has made the point that, in each of grades seven, eight, and nine, every student is to study one career cluster in depth. This will be of his own choosing—so that, if a youngster is drawn to business, he would do work in the business cluster for one year. His next interest might be hospitality and recreation, and he would concentrate in that area in the eighth grade. He might elect health careers in the ninth grade and spend his time entirely on that cluster. Then, in the tenth grade, he would select a course from one of these three clusters. This course would be one in which he would learn actual skills, so that he would be trained to handle a job in the field of his choosing. He would be taught the actual skills he would need so that, when he wanted to take a job, he would have them to offer to a prospective employer.

To repeat, in the seventh, eighth, or ninth grades, the young people would select the career clusters they were most interested in, and study them in depth, considering all of the careers that cluster has to offer.

This plan involves a number of details:

1. There must be fifteen career cluster courses offered, each of them one year long, and extensive in nature; the students must have the freedom to select the course and cluster in which they are most interested. This means that a large number of children may elect to take the same course; another course might not be quite as popular, and still another might have relatively few applicants. These are problems of administration, of course.

2. There is a decided lack of textbook material; the teachers and counselors handling the courses would have to virtually write their own curricula (an excellent idea, by the way, for people who are involved in their work). However, there are other sources of information which should be checked including newspapers, magazines, and brochures.

3. In an in-depth study as this is, actual on-the-spot visits are tremendously important. The more first-hand experiences the children can get, the better.

4. Where possible, "hands-on" experiences should be provided in the classroom. Actual work situations, for example, have more value than observing. In the State of Washington, where the emphasis on this type of teaching has existed for a number of years, children have run businesses, produced products, and have had a large number of experiences of this type.

The Office of Education is currently involved in listing the various careers within each cluster. You will find a summary of these listings in the Appendix of this book.

To use the curricula that follows, consider using it this way:

Each grade—seven, eight and nine—have five basic units to be covered by the class in about ten weeks. The remaining thirty weeks may be used to cover one career cluster of the youngster's choosing. Classes may be grouped according to the students' interests, and a student may spend the entire year working on a single cluster. In the event that this is done, each career within the cluster, or certainly as many as possible, should be investigated.

If actual working situations can be set up, these should be developed. The creative skills of the teacher and the career education resource person should be used to the fullest to develop a curriculum for the career cluster.

A SECOND APPROACH

We suggest that these three years be divided into two segments, unequal in length.

1. In the first segment, five basic areas are covered. These will differ for each grade, of course. Each one, however, is studied to give the students an understanding of the world of work and of career choice.

2. In the second segment, five career clusters are covered. If the child has already been introduced to the career clusters, this work will be covered in far greater depth than it was covered in the elementary school grades.

If the child is being presented with the material for the first time, he or she has a chance to become acquainted with the huge variety of careers from which it is possible to choose. Then, after the introduction, the particular careers in which each person is interested are studied. The method of study, however, differs considerably from that used in the elementary grades. We refer to it as career investigation, and it will be outlined fully later in this chapter.

A THIRD ALTERNATE APPROACH

If it is impossible for you to include the study of careers for three years, but one year can be devoted to it, you will find a method for doing this after the three-year curriculum is discussed. While it is obvious the children cannot learn as much in one year as in three, we believe very strongly that a one-year course will give them a basis for career choice and will orient their thinking so that they will, at least, have some idea of what the future may hold for them.

Here is a suggested curriculum for grades seven, eight, and nine that is based on the first alternate.

SEVENTH GRADE—SEGMENT ONE

Unit A. Questionnaire for seventh graders

The questionnaire that follows is suggested as the beginning of the Career Education Program for the seventh graders. It is a basis and a motivational device for the study of careers. It links the youngsters' current schooling with their future lives—which may or may not have been done for them before—and yet is extremely important. Tell the students this questionnaire is for their use. The results will be discussed in class, but the papers are confidential, and are the property of the boys and girls to retain in their career folders. Tell the children that this course is different from others, and that it is their opinions and their feelings which are of the greatest importance.

Career Education Questionnaire for the Seventh Grade

1. How old are you?
2. How many years have you been in school?
3. Do you think you have learned a great deal in this time?
4. Why or why not?
5. Do you think you have wasted some of your time?
6. Why or why not?
7. Why do you go to school?
8. In what way does school help you in your present life?
9. In what way will what you are learning help you in your future life?
10. Which subject or subjects do you think will help you most in your future life?
11. Which subject will be of the least value?
12. Would you come to school if you didn't have to come? Why?
13. How could school be made more meaningful for you?
14. What subjects would you like to take which you aren't taking now?
15. If you could have any career in the whole world, what career would you choose?

16. Actually, at this point, what career do you think you will have?

17. What reasons are you basing this on?

18. What educational preparation do you think this career requires?

19. What are some careers other than this one that you would consider?

20. What special talents do you have?

21. What are your best subjects in school?

22. Is it possible that any of these would lead to a career?

23. Do you have a hobby that might lead to a career? What?

24. Are you thinking of going to college? What course are you going to take? For what reason?

25. Are you one of the many people who need to learn about the very large variety of careers available to you?

Please emphasize to the students the need for truthful answers. Tell the boys and girls you will not collect these papers, that there is no need for them to put their names on them, and that they are for the sole purpose of helping the young people to learn more about themselves and what motivates them.

When the questionnaires have been completed, go over the responses.

The first two questions are to "loosen the children up" a bit, and get them into the swing of answering questions.

Numbers three, four, five, and six are to get an idea of how the student feels about himself in relation to school. Number seven is a very critical question, since all too often we have found children do not see any connection between their schooling and their future lives. Unless we help the children to become aware of the value of education and its effect on their future lives, our efforts to educate them often prove futile.

Questions eight, nine, ten, eleven, and twelve give further insight into the child's feelings about his education. Question thirteen is a very important one, as is fourteen. Question fifteen is one that the young people like, and one which almost lets them get this idea out of their systems. Question sixteen is an attempt at realistic thinking, seventeen tries to unearth the thought processes behind the career choice; and eighteen and nineteen show how much actual knowledge the student has in this area. Questions twenty through twenty-four attempt to help the student to look at his talents and abilities. Twenty-five is included to show this particular student he is not alone.

Discuss the students' replies, pointing out the value of education, the need for realistic thinking, and the need for information about various careers. Use this to lead into the second unit, "Why do people work?"

Unit B. Why do people work?

Concepts to be covered

People work for a variety of reasons:

1. The most obvious reason is to earn the money they need to purchase the basic necessities of life—food, shelter, and clothing. They also will want to purchase other things as well.

2. Many people work to make their lives interesting. An elected official is a multi-millionaire, yet he chooses to work rather than be unemployed.)

3. When one works, he or she can and should look for a career that meets his or her needs. If one needs excitement, he or she should look for a career that has it. If one needs prestige, one should seek a career that offers it.

4. A great many people work to keep active. Of course, a person can be active even after he retires, but for some it is better to work than to retire.

5. If one has chosen the right career, it will bring that person job satisfaction—the feeling of doing a good job, of being appreciated, and of contributing to the common good. The poet John Donne said it beautifully, "No man is an island," and, indeed, each person through his career and his personal life can help others as he helps himself.

Activities

1. Have children discuss with their parents the costs of living in terms of their immediate needs. Discuss this in your class. (Very often children have no idea how much it costs to support a household. They need some understanding of this if they are to study salaries when they do research on various occupations.) Have pupils use newspaper advertisements to study the costs of rentals, food, and clothing. List some of these for a family of four. (Figuring may be done for a single person, too.)

2. Have the class read biographies of people whose work

brought them a great deal of satisfaction as well as fame—Thomas A. Edison, or George Washington Carver, for example. Then have children relate the lives of these people to people alive and working today.

3. Have each child interview three people he knows who work, asking:

     a. What is the main reason they work?
     b. What other reasons do they have for working?
     c. Does their job bring them satisfaction?
     d. If they could do it again, would they change their career, or select the same one? Why?

4. Have children form buzz groups, discuss the following topic among themselves: What kind of career would bring me job satisfaction?

After they have discussed this, have them each write a paragraph on the topic. Tell them to put this away and that it will be referred to later on in the year.

Unit C. Why should women as well as men plan for a career?

Concepts

Women make up an increasing percentage of the nation's work force. Some work before marriage. Others work until their children are born. Still others return to work after the children are in school. Some women never marry and support themselves. There are those families in which the husband has been injured and cannot work or in which there is no father. In such families the mother must work to earn money for the needs of the family. Other women will work to bring in extra money so that the family may enjoy things it could not afford otherwise.

Women may choose to work because they become bored staying at home and wish to utilize their talents. Still others want to make a contribution to society, and may begin their careers relatively late in life.

If you are a woman, the chances are you will want to have a career some time in your life. If you are trained for a particular career area, you are far better off than the woman who must take an unskilled job—or the one who must get training long after her teens.

A great number of career areas are opening up for women which were never available before.

Activities

1. Take a poll. Ask children to think of all of the women they know. How many work? Remind them their mothers may work at home now. How many worked outside the home before they had families? How many plan to work again?

2. Invite a "career woman" to speak to the group. Try to choose a woman in a field other than teaching or nursing (since these are the two fields most frequently associated with women).

Have the class prepare the questions it will ask in advance. For example:

"Why did you decide on this career?"

"Have you had difficulty in it because you are a woman?"

"Has your career interfered with your family life?"

3. Have class check newspapers and magazines for articles about careers which are relatively new to women. Make a bulletin board display of these.

4. Discuss the "Women's Lib" movement in terms of the right for equal wages for the same jobs, equal opportunities for women, and day-care centers for working mothers.

5. Have children make a list of the growing number of careers available to women. Encourage them to draw on their own knowledge to do this.

You may wish to have them make a montage of pictures of women at work. Photos may be cut from magazines. Drawings and cartoons may be done by the children.

Unit D. Why should a person select a career cluster, rather than a specific career?

Concepts

A career cluster includes a group of careers. These are all related, in that they contain similar elements. However, they are also different and because of this, one may be able to find the particular career that suits him or her exactly. There are careers that require four or more years of training or education, and those that require considerably less. Of course, the careers requiring the more intensive and longer education will enable the person to earn much more money than the person with less training. Yet these careers are all to be found within one career cluster. Therefore, by selecting a career cluster first, there are many careers to choose from. Then, later on, one particular career is selected—the one which is best suited to the person—which best meets his needs, and best suits his personality.

Let us say a person decides he or she wants to enter a health career. He or she may choose any career—from being a nurse's aide, for which there is often on-the-job training, to becoming a psychoanalyst, for which one must spend years at special universities after he or she graduates from college. Yet both the nurse's aide and the psychoanalyst are careers to be found within the health career cluster.

Fifteen different career clusters will be studied, with a large number of career opportunities within each.

Keeping an open mind is one of the most important aspects of the study of careers. If a student is to gain as much as he can from it, he must be ready to really think about the information with which he is presented—and apply it to himself. People often change their minds while still in school, or change their careers after they have tried them.

Activities

1. List the fifteen career clusters on the board:
   Agri-business and Natural Resources
   Business and Office
   Communication and Media
   Construction
   Consumer and Homemaking Education
   Environment
   Fine Arts and Humanities
   Health
   Hospitality and Recreation
   Manufacturing
   Marine Science
   Marketing and Distribution
   Personal Services
   Public Service
   Transportation

Have the children select one or two of these clusters and suggest careers to fit within them. Or you may have them fit in as many careers within each cluster as they are able to. (This will depend on their backgrounds and how much they have learned about careers in elementary school.)

2. You may wish to do a bulletin board, showing the various clusters, with some of the careers illustrated below. Try to include careers on all levels—from unskilled through professional.

3. Have the class secretary write to the National Association of Home Builders, 1625 L Street N.W., Washington, D.C. 20036, for their booklet, *The Young People's Guide to Home Building* by John Q. Builder. This booklet will give them an idea of the roles played by the various craftsmen in the building of a house. These are all careers in the construction cluster.

4. Divide the class into buzz groups. Have each group discuss the following points and report back to the class:

    a. What do I think is important as far as a career is concerned?

    b. Do I want to start work immediately after high school, or get additional training? Why?

    c. What career clusters could a person go into who wants to help other people?

    d. What career clusters offer opportunities for people to go into business for themselves?

Unit E. What are the different levels of employment and how do they affect the salary a person earns?

Concepts

Levels of employment have been divided into five basic areas:

1. Unskilled level—physical work that requires a person to use his strength and muscles; few skills are involved.

2. Semiskilled level—work that involves the knowledge of some skills. Often these skills are learned on-the-job to suit the needs of the particular employer.

3. Skilled level—work that involves a large number of definite skills, which may be learned in vocational school or through an apprenticeship program.

4. Technical level—work which involves the knowledge of a large number of highly specialized skills, which may be learned in a technical institute or in a college.

5. Professional or managerial—work that involves a great many skills enabling a person to supervise others. This generally requires four or more years of college preparation.

Activities

1. Discuss each level in terms of careers within it. Have children

cite examples. Then add to these. Here are some samples of careers within the employment levels:

Unskilled:	Ditch digger
	Elevator operator
	Delivery man
	Paper boy
	Service station attendant
Semiskilled:	Factory machine operator
	Factory product inspector
	Postal clerk
	Bakery worker
	Laundry worker
Skilled:	Engraver
	Carpenter
	Crane operator
	Beautician
	Practical nurse
Technician:	Medical technician
	Radio and television technician
	Engineering technician
	Air conditioning technician
	Dental technician
Professional:	Engineer
	Teacher
	Nurse
	Meteorologist
	Architect

2. Speakers may be invited to discuss their personal careers in terms of opportunities within their career levels.

3. In discussing salaries, have the children use the help-wanted ads in the local newspaper. (If your community is a small one, use the paper of the largest city nearby.)

Select a series of careers and have the children look up the salaries paid.

4. Use the following graphs with them:

Have them compare the incomes of people with unskilled jobs with the incomes of college-trained people.

5. Point out the need for technically trained people. If possible, draw this conclusion from evidence in the advertisements.

6. Discuss the disappearance of unskilled jobs. You may wish to

LIFETIME INCOME GROWS As EDUCATIONAL LEVELS RISE

YEARS of SCHOOL COMPLETED	1968 LIFETIME INCOME FOR MEN—AGE 18 To DEATH
TOTAL	$ 357,552
ELEM.—LESS THAN 8 YRS.	213,505
8 YEARS	276,755
H.S. — 1 To 3 YEARS	308,305
4 YEARS	371,094
COLLEGE — 1 To 3 YEARS	424,280
4 YEARS or MORE	607,921
4 YEARS	584,062
5 YRS. or MORE	636,119

Occupational Outlook Handbook 1974-75; U.S. Dept. of Labor

cite as examples the elevator operator, the dishwasher, and the pin boy who sets up the pins in bowling alleys. Have the children think of other examples.

SEVENTH GRADE—SEGMENT TWO

In this segment, it is suggested the following career clusters be studied in depth. Approximately two months should be devoted to each cluster, with the remaining time for review.

Construction
Transportation
Hospitality and Recreation
Health
Consumer and Homemaking

The young people will learn far more if the exploratory method is used. The career investigation that follows is one technique that you will find useful. It gives them the entire responsibility for the task at hand.

We suggest you discuss the career cluster first in general terms.

You will find a listing of many of the careers included in it in the Appendix. Then you may divide the class into committees to study the individual careers, or you may have each student investigate the career area in which he is most interested.

DOING A CAREER INVESTIGATION

You may rexograph forms for this, or an outline of the format to be used.

1. Title—the particular career area, for example plumber, dentist, radio technician, or supermarket manager.

2. Job description—exactly what tasks are involved in the career? What does the person do on a day-to-day, hour-to-hour basis? Which tasks are repeated? Which tasks are done occasionally?

3. What are the salaries paid?

4. What is the training or education necessary?

5. How can a person finance this education?

6. What are the current markets for this career in your locality?

7. What are the advantages of this career area?

8. What are the disadvantages?

9. What are my reasons for an interest in this area?

10. What are related careers? This information is important because if a person starts to work in this area, he might want to work his way up to another career. Another reason is that if he found he did not like this career, he might move into another.

The job description may be found in many publications. The *Dictionary of Occupational Titles,* the *Encyclopedia of Careers,* and the *Occupational Outlook Handbook* are three resources, but there are many more. Incidentally, these books will also help the investigator to answer the questions which follow.

There are many other sources for obtaining the information to answer these questions. These include interviews with people pursuing the career, the advertisements in the local newspapers, and discussions with personnel managers and with employment counselors.

THE FINAL ACTIVITIES OF EACH CLUSTER

1. At the completion of the unit, do the following as a class activity. Do it carefully and spend adequate time on it.

   a. List the careers according to levels of employment—unskilled, semiskilled, skilled, technical, and professional. This involves selecting those careers that are within each category. Have the students do the actual listing.

b. Discuss the education and training necessary for each of these careers, and then the salaries paid in each.

c. You will find certain clusters where there are many unskilled and semiskilled workers. There are others where these are relatively few in number. Then, on the opposite end of the continuum, there are clusters where there are very few professionals and others where there are many.

d. Discuss obvious advantages and disadvantages, in terms of the entire cluster. (In the construction cluster, for instance, many jobs are seasonal, because it is difficult to build during the winter.)

2. List the careers for which there are job openings in your community. Check with the guidance counselor or career education coordinator for assistance in obtaining this information. *Make this one of the most important aspects of the unit.*

Point out to those students who are interested in a career in this cluster where they might apply for summer or part-time jobs so that they can sample the career first hand. For most jobs they will be too young, but instruct them to use this knowledge later to help them determine whether or not this should be their first career.

If there are no jobs available, point that out. However, consider the point that job opportunities do change from year to year. Nevertheless, if there haven't been any for a number of years, the choice is a poor one.

CULMINATING THE YEAR'S WORK

There are a number of ways in which this culmination may be done:

1. Hold a career fair, at which time the reports the children have prepared and the remainder of the work they have done are put on display. This might include pictures taken on visits to places of employment and montages of photographs of a particular career.

Divide the class into committees and have each prepare a particular career area for presentation. Then have each group discuss the career. Or you may divide the class into committees, assign a career cluster to each, and have them discuss the large variety of careers within that cluster.

This type of activity is excellent for presentation to the parents. Should you wish to invite speakers for the fair, you may do so. Plan to have an audience of parents, and possibly children from the lower grades in your school or from neighboring elementary schools.

2. Have the children prepare a career book or a newspaper. This, too, can serve as a review of the work that has been done for the term. It has the added advantage of providing review material, which the children retain as their personal property.

The book might consist of a collection of their reports, or, if the volume is too large, of summaries of each of them.

3. Review, in some fashion, the work the young people have covered during the year. We hope to have them retain as much of it as possible, and reviewing will reinforce the material you have covered with them and reveal any of the areas that require additional information.

GRADE EIGHT—SEGMENT ONE

We feel about ten weeks should be allotted to this portion of the work. However, as with everything that follows, the length of time to be spent on a particular topic will depend on the class and on the teacher.

Unit A. Self-awareness of one's talents, strengths, abilities, and lack of abilities.

It is essential that the child have some idea of his own talents, strengths, and abilities—and also of the areas in which he is deficient. The latter should not be brought up to discourage him, but to help him realistically survey the situation.

Because many children are totally unrealistic when it comes to the entire subject of careers and career choice, we must ask that you, the teacher, stress a need to be aware of things as they are, and not as we would want them to be. A child who has done poorly in academic subjects all through school will probably experience difficulty in high school, and, if he ever reaches college, there, too. It is dishonest not to discuss this—not with the child, specifically, but in general, with the entire class and privately with individual children, if you feel this is necessary.

However, it is our belief that most children sell themselves short. They do not reach high enough. Their aspirations depend on many factors, especially the influence of their parents and friends.

We believe one of our goals, as teachers, should be to help each child strive to reach his potential, or at least approach it.

The questionnaire that follows will help each person pinpoint some aspects of his own personality. It is designed to encourage each person to think of himself as an individual who has different likes, dislikes, strengths, and weaknesses.

After the questionnaire has been filled out, we suggest you go over it. We will discuss specifically how below.

"Getting to Know Yourself" Questionnaire

1. What is your name?
2. How old are you now?
3. Do you like to be with people?
4. If you had your choice, would you select a job that puts you in contact with others?
5. Would you prefer to work alone?
6. Would you like to work in an atmosphere of excitement?
7. Do you enjoy meeting people you have never met before?
8. Can you take orders from others?
9. Does working under pressure upset you?
10. Do you like to work with children?
11. Would you like to work with small groups of either adults or children?
12. Would you like to help people who are sick?
13. Can you stand the sight of blood, or of a person bleeding, or would this make you ill?
14. Do you like being in a hospital atmosphere?
15. Do you particularly enjoy playing with animals?
16. Would you like to work with animals?
17. Do you feel you have patience?
18. Would you like a job which keeps you out-of-doors?
19. Do you react well to very hot or very cold weather?
20. Are you interested in nature and living things?
21. Are you physically strong?
22. Would you care to do work using this strength?
23. Do you think you would be able to stand on your feet all day?
24. Do you like to fix things?
25. Are you interested in cars or machines?
26. Do you enjoy doing work that requires you to be very exact?

27. Do you get satisfaction from creating things?

28. Do you get a feeling of accomplishment from making something work that has broken down?

29. Do people often tell you, "You ought to be a lawyer?"

30. Do you enjoy talking to people who are older than you?

31. Would you rather talk than read?

32. Do you often work on projects?

33. Do you come up with new ideas?

34. Did you ever spend much time planning?

35. Did things work out the way you planned them?

36. Can you plan one thing, and then do another—if you see a reason for the change?

37. Do you feel you have a special talent in art, music, dance, dramatics, sewing, woodworking or ceramics?

38. Can that talent be applied to a career?

39. Would you want to devote your life to cultivating that talent?

40. Can you see a practical use for that talent?

41. What is the subject you enjoy most in school? Why?

42. What is the subject you are best in?

43. Can you think of any careers based on this subject? What are they?

44. Do you think you would like to choose a career based on this subject? Why?

45. Are you interested in finding a career related to language arts? Have you any ideas—if so, what are they?

46. Are you interested in improving the health of human beings and other living things?

47. Do you enjoy working with numbers?

48. Are you interested in solving problems involving numbers?

49. Are you interested in a career in the business world? Why?

50. Do you feel you have absolutely no ideas now about possible careers?

51. Do you want to go to college? Why?

52. As of now, do you think your past marks indicate you would be able to go on to college and graduate?

53. In what type of job do you think you would be happy?

54. If you had to think of one outstanding character trait in regard to yourself, what would that be?

55. At this point in your life, if you could have any career in the world you wanted, what would that be?

56. Do you think you could ever have that career? Why, or why not?

57. In what career or job do you think you will actually earn your living? Why?

After they have completed the questionnaire, tell the children: "This questionnaire is designed to help you to learn some things about your personality. It certainly won't tell you everything there is to know. In fact, it really only scratches the surface. But it does give you some ideas. We will be discussing these."

Then discuss the following topics:

1. If a person likes to be with people, what are some of the careers he might choose?

2. If a person prefers to work alone, or with a few people, what are possible careers?

3. What do we mean by "working under pressure"? What careers are "pressure cookers"?

4. What connection has the ability to take orders with career choice?

5. Why can the ability to stand the sight of blood be a factor in choosing a career?

6. What factors should one consider if he or she wishes to work out-of-doors?

Go over the entire questionnaire, discussing its various aspects, and linking the items with career choice.

Point out even those aspects that may seem obvious—such as the fact that a person who is introverted would be happier as a librarian than as a teacher.

Make your discussion as practical as possible. The knowledge you are going to instill will affect the children's lives.

Unit B. Education and training for a career determines the career level

Review the material covered in Unit E of the seventh grade curriculum, which covers levels of employment. Then correlate that with the following information:

1. Most unskilled work requires little or no training. People are told what is expected of them on the job. Nevertheless, some unskilled jobs ask that the applicant be a high school graduate. This is not true of every unskilled job, but of many of them.

2. Semiskilled careers involve simple skills which are most often taught to the person on the job, and this is referred to as "on-the-job training." Operators are people who operate machines in factories

and who receive their training on the machine they will use. This training may require a few hours, a few days, or sometimes a few months.

3. Skilled workers are people who have spent long periods of time learning the skills they use. They may have learned them in high schools or in special vocational schools. Another form of education for skilled workers is through apprenticeships, which are a combination of work and schooling. Apprenticeships may require a long period of time—such as four to six years, but the person earns while he learns. Then, too, there are skilled workers who have learned all their skills on the job over a period of years.

4. Technical careers are prepared for by attending either technical schools, sometimes called institutes, or two-year (community) colleges where career courses are offered.

5. Professional careers are prepared for by attending college for at least four or more years.

6. Careers as managers are prepared for by a combination of college training (usually), and experience (without question) in a particular field.

Activities

1. To show the connection between job earnings and education, select a series of careers (have the students suggest them) and check the help-wanted advertisements for salaries. (If they are not available there, check with your State Employment Office.) It may be necessary to consult the pages of a paper in a large city in your area if there are insufficient advertisements in your local newspaper.

2. Use the graph previously illustrated which shows the statistics on a nationwide basis. (Incidentally, these figures were the latest available. Incomes have gone up—but proportionally.) We usually refer to this graph as the "Education Pays" graph.

3. Have the students determine the number of openings there are for unskilled workers and for semiskilled operators. Review with them the concept that many unskilled careers are being phased out by modern technology.

4. If possible, invite several speakers from various levels of employment, asking them to compare their careers in terms of what they actually do during the course of a day, what salaries a person doing this type of work might expect (stress you are not asking what *they* earn), and what the opportunities for advancement are.

5. Discuss apprenticeship programs. Contact several of the local

unions for information about the programs in your area. Invite a speaker to explain exactly what these programs are, and how a person applies for one.

6. Arrange for the class to visit a technical school. Ask that someone well acquainted with the school describe the various programs to the students and show them the school buildings.

7. Do the same for a four-year college.

Please remember not to denigrate any career as your youngsters study this unit. However, make sure they understand the value of education or training in terms of earning a living and in terms of an interesting life. College is not for every student, but some type of training should be.

Unit C. The career ladder concept—where one enters a career ladder depends on his or her training or education, plus the availability of jobs.

The career ladder concept may be defined in this way: each career area or industry offers a variety of jobs, ranging from unskilled jobs through professional careers. A person may determine by the amount of educational preparation he receives by what level on the career ladder he will enter the career area. The level at which he enters will determine his salary.

For example, let us look at the career area of office occupations. Unskilled workers are often file clerks or mail handlers. Semiskilled careers involve payroll clerks or switchboard operators. Business machine operators or secretaries may be considered skilled workers. Bookkeepers or keypunch operators would be technicians. The accountant is one professional within the office occupations.

The career ladder varies from career area to career area. No two are exactly alike. However, the principle holds true that the more skills a person has learned, the more salary he will earn, and the more chance he has for advancement.

Activities

1. Discuss the career ladder concept, and work out the ladder for several career areas.

Have the class work out diagrams showing this for example:

<pre>
                                            Accountant
                              Bookkeeper
                   Secretary
              Switchboard
     File   Operator
     Clerk
</pre>

2. Divide the class into committees, and have each committee elect a secretary. Instruct the secretary to write to one two-year college and one four-year college or institute selected by the group for their catalogs.

Instruct each committee to study the catalog and list the careers for which a student at that college might prepare.

3. Have the class select help-wanted advertisements for a series of levels on a career ladder. Indicate the salaries earned on each level. Calculate the value in dollars and cents per year of education or training.

4. Invite a builder to discuss the various levels of employment as they exist in the construction industry. Ask him to discuss the salaries earned on each level.

5. Point out the fact that a person may find job satisfaction on any level. For example, for a person who loves animals, there are careers ranging from aides in animal hospitals to technicians and then to veterinarians. What career ladder might be open to people who want to help others? To people who want to do research?

Unit D. Financing One's Education

In our country there are a number of ways to finance one's education. High school education is, of course, without charge if one goes to a public high school. As far as education after high school is concerned, there are a number of ways to finance college or vocational school.

1. There are city and state colleges, both two- and four-year, which have lowered fees. The community colleges, for example, are comparatively inexpensive. If the course you are interested in is offered you can get your education very inexpensively. Many two-year courses at community colleges are career oriented—that is, you are trained in specific skills and you can begin your career in that field after two years of free education.

2. Private and state colleges and universities often offer scholarships and grants. Some are for full tuition; others are for partial tuition. You apply for a scholarship or grant after you were accepted by the college.

3. Students who wish to attend accredited colleges or vocational schools may borrow money from local banks. These loans are called student loans, and are not expected to be repaid until after the student graduates, nor is there any interest charged until after graduation. Anyone who is accepted for college or technical or vocational training can apply for such a loan.

4. Many young people have one of the above sources of income,

and also work at jobs within the college or the community. Others work their way through school, completely paying for themselves.

5. Some families pay the student's expenses.

Whatever way you decide upon, you can get the funds you need to get posthigh school training. When he was President, Lyndon Johnson said, "No person has to be denied a college education because of lack of funds." The same is true of vocational training. While the exact conditions included here may change, there will be money available, we believe, for posthigh school education.

Activities

1. Because of the importance of this topic, spend as much time as necessary discussing it, making sure the children understand it fully. In the discussion take up actual cases, brothers and sisters, other relatives, and friends. How did they pay for their education after high school? Bring the discussion as close to home as possible.

2. Bring to class a copy of Feinberg's book on scholarships. Have children read it, selecting ones which are applicable or unusual. You will find both in this book. Another source is the American Legion's fine booklet on the subject called "Need a Lift?"

Point out the important role the guidance counselor can play in helping students to obtain scholarships.

3. Have each of the students send for a technical school or college catalog. Then have the class draw up a comparison of the costs at all of the schools or colleges for which they have information.

Include nontuition schools and colleges, such as those run by the city or state, as well as private colleges.

4. Using the catalogs, have the students figure out which courses are offered at the nontuition schools and which at the schools where tuition is charged. Make a composite listing of this information.

5. Take the class on a trip to nearby schools and colleges. If facilities are available for travel, visit as many as possible, including both tuition and nontuition-charging schools.

Arrange, if possible, to have some person at the college, preferably someone young, talk with the group, giving information about the school and about the students.

DO NOT EXCLUDE ANY YOUNGSTER FROM THIS TYPE OF TRIP BECAUSE YOU THINK HE OR SHE MAY NEVER SEEK EDUCATION AFTER HIGH SCHOOL. On the contrary, encourage participation in such trips for every child in the class.

Unit E. The concept of the back-up career

Many pupils will choose careers that are difficult to enter and in which success is often elusive. For those pupils we must enforce the concept of the back-up career. Discuss the following story with the class:

Bob Jones has his heart set on being a professional baseball player. He is a good ballplayer now, but he is only fourteen years of age and his future development is uncertain. However, he loves baseball and is very anxious to make this his life's work. He is a good student.

How should he plan his future?

1. Point out to the students that Bob cannot really prepare for a career in baseball on a full-time basis. He will continue to play on both the school team and his neighborhood team, but he cannot study baseball in school.

2. Ask them: "What would happen if Bob hasn't improved very much by the time he graduates? He isn't good enough to go on. What should he do?"

3. Are there any courses Bob could take which might help him?

4. What will Bob have to do if, when he graduates, he is unable to get a job playing ball?

5. Most ball players are over eighteen when they begin playing professional ball. What might Bob do in the meantime?

6. If Bob were to go to college, what subject might he major in?

7. How else, besides playing ball, might he use this major? (Bring out the idea he might teach health education, or become a camp counselor. Eventually he might become a coach. Teaching and coaching would be his back-up careers.)

Activities

1. Have the class define the concept clearly: If there is some question as to whether or not one will be able to go into the career of one's first choice, one should choose a second career. Like a back-up pilot, who flies a mission if the first pilot cannot, the back-up career is in the wings waiting, but only if the first career doesn't work out.

Have the class list a number of careers which should have back-ups. Be sure they include careers in the entertainment field or in professional sports. This is also true of such careers as modeling, airline stewardesses, and pilots. It pertains to the arts, as well, because it is difficult to make a living as a beginning painter or sculptor, for example. The same is true of becoming an author or poet.

2. Teaching is often chosen as a back-up career. Have the students ask a number of their teachers if teaching was their first choice or a back-up. They will probably find one or more for whom it was the back-up. Ask for further information about this.

3. Ask the students to interview their parents and other adults to see if there are people who had to use a second career because their first choice did not work out.

4. Have the pupils read the autobiographies of famous people in a variety of fields. These usually bring out the need for an inordinate amount of perserverance. Discuss this with the youngsters.

5. Many times young people have a distorted idea of what a career actually involves. Have them discuss this from the information they learn by reading the autobiographies. Discuss the work of the stewardesses, or of second-string professional ballplayers.

EIGHTH GRADE—SEGMENT TWO

In this segment, it is suggested the following career clusters be studied in depth, allowing approximately two months for each cluster (if this is a year-long course). Use the career investigation described earlier in this chapter, the material on utilizing the career investigation, and culminating the year's work.

The career clusters for the eighth grade are:

Agri-business and natural Resources
Business and Office
Communication and Media
Manufacturing
Personal Services

Additional material for this study will be found in the Appendix.

NINTH GRADE—SEGMENT ONE

Unit A. Questionnaire: Where do your abilities, talents, and interests lie?

(Stress that this is confidential and for the students' personal use only.)

1. Have you done any work that interests you? If so, what type of work is that?

2. Can you analyze what it is about that work that you enjoy? If you didn't enjoy it, can you figure out what it is about it that you didn't enjoy?

3. If you had to make one statement about your future life's work, what would that be?

4. Are you primarily interested in earning a good living?

5. Are you primarily interested in having time for leisure activities?

6. Are you primarily interested in helping other people?

7. Are you primarily interested in a career that offers advancement?

8. Are you able to take orders from other people, or is it important that you be your own boss?

9. Are you able to accept responsibility?

10. Do you like going to school? Do you plan to go to college?

11. Have you been able to pass every subject?

12. If you are a young woman, are you planning on preparing for a career?

13. Have you thought of any career toward which, at this point, you feel drawn?

14. If so, why are you drawn toward it?

15. Is there any particular subject in which you excel? If so, what is it? Can you think of any career associated with it which might be good for you?

16. Is there any talent you have which might lead you into a career? If so, what is that?

17. Is the career area you have chosen one which requires a back-up career? If so, have you chosen one? What?

18. Does your personality suit the career area you are thinking about? In what ways?

19. Do you have to overcome any handicap, personality-wise or physically, to achieve this career? Why?

20. What careers have you studied that appeal to you? Why?

21. Select one career now, for the purposes of this questionnaire. (This is for yourself. No one else will read it.) What is that career?

22. What type of education or training do you need for it?

23. How will you be able to pay for that education or training?

24. Why did you choose that career area?

If you wish to go over this questionnaire, please respect the children's confidentiality. However, you will find some who are willing or anxious to discuss their responses.

Point out that this questionnaire may be used again in the future to help zero in on a career area, and that there are still many careers the students have not studied. Furthermore, there are new careers developing every day, such as careers in environmental science.

Point out that in the ninth grade you will be discussing the selection of a career area, rather than a particular career. Review the concept of the career cluster and the career ladder.

Remind the students to think in terms of themselves as they study the material in this year's work. Are they interested in a career in any of these areas? If so, why? If not, why not? What is it about the career area they like? What don't they like?

Unit B. Clues to selecting a career

Using the results of the questionnaire, develop first the concept of one's personality (the term we give to a person's behavior and other people's reactions to it). Discuss various aspects of personality such as the ability to communicate readily with one's peers, with older persons, with children. Other aspects include:

- The ability to concentrate on work in spite of many distractions.
- The need for a great deal of privacy.
- The ability to smile and be pleasant most of the time.
- The desire to please other people.
- The ability to take orders.
- The ability to give orders.

Point out that it is a person's personality that makes him unique, and which will have a tremendous effect on his career. Therefore, it should be taken into consideration as he selects that career. Have the children list other qualities they can think of that fit into this area called personality.

Next talk about the person who cannot think of a single career area he likes. Why is this true? Point out that there are usually some drawbacks to every choice but that, once a choice is made, this is more helpful to the student than if he goes through his life saying, "I just can't decide what I want to be."

Activities

1. Have the pupils describe the personality of a person who

would be successful in a particular career. Have them choose the career area first. This may be an actual person or a fictitious case they develop.

Have these descriptions read aloud. This activity can be made very interesting by collecting the papers (with no names on them) and then having one person read them. After they are discussed, have the children try to guess who wrote each.

2. Next select a person who is successful in his or her career, and try to analyze what it is that makes him or her successful. (This may very well be a member of the school staff, but not necessarily. It may also be a famous person. Remember, though, to bring out the fact that many famous people are not happy.)

3. Have the pupils interview people they know whom they consider successful, again trying to decide what it is about their personalities which helped them. (You may wish to tell the story of the millionaire who went to a college reunion. A friend met him, and said, after hearing about the gentleman's activities, "Well, you always were very lucky." "You're right," the millionaire replied, "but I must say one thing. The harder I work, the luckier I am.")

4. Have the pupils think about the following areas in terms of themselves:

    a. Am I a good student? Do I get good grades? If I decide to go to college, will I be able to make it? Would I be wiser to choose a career that doesn't require college training?

    b. Do I like going to school? If I plan on going to college, should I select a two- or a four-year program? Do I have a good chance of completing it? Am I willing to do the work necessary—knowing in advance that there will be a lot of work?

    c. Am I willing to work hard in high school, so that I will have the grades necessary to be accepted in college? (Note: The ninth grade is an excellent time to discuss this particular topic.)

    d. Do I like working with people, or would I prefer a job that removes me from face-to-face contact with others?

    e. Would I choose to work with children if I had the chance?

    f. Would I be happier working out of doors if I could do so?

    g. Do I enjoy being part of the business world, working in retailing, for example?

    h. How do I react to a situation where I must make decisions constantly?

    i. How do I react to a situation where I have to solve problems all the time?

    j. Do I enjoy helping people?

    k. Do I particularly want to work with animals?

    l. Do I particularly want to work with plants?

    m. Do I want to create things?

    n. Does any talent I have warrant my planning a career around it?

All of these questions lead to possible clues to career choice. Keep them in mind as you continue your study of careers. Also use them to think about career areas you have already studied.

Unit C. Following through—from selecting a career to being successful in it.

If one is to benefit from career development, the first thing that must be realized is that this is a continuous process. It begins with the selection of a career area based on ability, interest, or talent. It continues with preparation for that career. This is followed by searching for and finding a job in that career area. The next step is succeeding in that job. Possibly another step might be advancing from that career to another. The last step would be retirement.

No one is to say that a person must stay in the same career all his life. Many people have had several careers, and these are among the most successful individuals. However, it is essential that each person begin somewhere in the world of work. It is up to you to select the point at which you wish to start, and then follow through.

Activities

1. Have each student select a career, even if it is not one in which he or she is very interested. He or she is selecting it only to learn how the follow-through process works. However, ask the student to give reasons for his choice, based on the concepts studied earlier this term. These include personality, academic strengths as evidenced by school work, and talents and outside interests.

Encourage the students to verbalize their reasons for this choice. Stress, however, the concept that this career choice is being made for the purposes of further study.

Now have each student work out plans for obtaining the education he would need for this career. Where would he attend high school? What courses would he or she take? Would he or she have to go to college? What courses would be taken? Would a vocational or technical school or an institute be better? Could the student take an apprenticeship after high school?

Have all the possibilities explored, including a variety of colleges. Include both tuition-free and private colleges.

Next, have the student consider how he or she would pay for this education. (Remember this is highly personal material that must be kept confidential. This topic was covered in the eighth grade, but should be reviewed. It is extremely important, so please make sure the youngsters understand it fully.) Encourage the boys and girls to be honest with themselves. You may wish to point out that, for most careers, tuition-free education is available. This is very different from years ago, due to the development of the community colleges. Higher education has been placed within the reach of anyone who wants it.

2. Arrange visits for the class to nearby colleges, as suggested for the eighth grade. If the other activities listed in that grade have not been carried out, or if you wish to do so again, repeat them. They are an essential aspect of career education.

3. Invite speakers from nearby colleges to address the class, pointing out the various programs available. Ask the speakers, however, to consider careers rather than college majors. In other words, ask them to discuss occupations rather than academic areas of study.

4. Invite a high school or college guidance counselor to discuss scholarships and grants. Try to choose a person who is interested, and has a wide knowledge of the subject.

5. Invite a representative of your local bank to discuss student loans.

6. Have the students compare scholarships, loans, and tuition-free education.

Point out that there are some careers for which one must attend a university that charges tuition. Dental college is only one example. It is for this situation that student loans are particularly good.

Unit D. Succeeding in high school and in posthigh school education

In order to succeed in high school and in any school one attends after high school, there are a number of aspects every student should consider:

1. Planning and making choices. Every student should begin by making plans. Of course, these are flexible and can easily be changed. However, even a temporary plan is far better than none.

Planning involves making choices. However, these selections are made simpler if there is a plan to guide one. For example, if a student plans to go to college, he or she must take the courses in high school that college requires. When it comes to deciding which foreign language to take, that choice is not affected too much by the master plan, so another decision must be made.

2. Accepting responsibility for one's actions. This covers a great deal of ground, from doing one's work to one's personal conduct in regard to daily living.

In junior high school, most pupils have far less responsibility than in high school. By the time they get to college they have even more. A willingness to accept this responsibility and to handle it maturely will make the difference between success and failure in school.

Activities

1. Discuss with the class the following topics:
   a. What planning have you ever done for yourself?
   b. What responsibilities do you have now?
   c. Which responsibilities were assigned to you? Which did you assume yourself?
   d. Do you think it important for young people to have responsibilities? Why?
   e. Whose responsibility should career planning be?
   f. Where is help available for career planning?

2. Invite a number of graduates from your school back to talk with the students. Divide the class into groups and ask one of the graduates to talk with each group about planning, making choices, and accepting responsibility. Have the students work out a series of questions to ask, so that these talks will be fruitful.

3. Invite a college guidance counselor to discuss why young people drop out of high school or college. Then have the students relate what has been said to people they know, or possibly to themselves.

4. Ask each student to write a paragraph or two on how he has planned his future life. This should be kept confidential, of course, but after the papers have been written they should be discussed in the class in abstract terms.

Ask for a volunteer to read his paper and then ask the entire class to judge whether the person is being realistic. If no one volunteers, use the following. It's the statement of one young man:

"I plan to go to high school and then to college. I want to study oceanography because I am very interested in science and in the ocean.

I realize I might have trouble getting a job, so I will also prepare for a career teaching science in college.

I will be able to go to XYZ Community College for my first two years, and then to ABC, which also is tuition free. In that way my family will not have to spend a great deal of money on my education.

There's also another possibility. I might get married—and let my wife help me."

Unit E. Finding and getting started on that first job

There are a number of techniques to cover with your students in terms of looking for a job. These hold true whether it is a summer job or a permanent one after they have received the training they need to pursue a particular career:

A. Finding the job:

1. Talk to everyone you know, asking if they know about any job opening, or if they know someone who knows someone.

2. Follow up any lead you find, no matter how slight it may appear to be.

3. Answer help-wanted advertisements in your local newspaper.

4. Check out the employment agencies—both private and the State Employment Service.

5. Pound the pavements, or cement yourself to the telephone, but contact many employers personally. Small businessmen often need help which they do not advertise for because of the expense.

6. File applications everywhere you possibly can.

7. Learn about opportunities in civil service—working for the city, state or Federal government.

8. Stick to your guns if you are looking for a first job in a particular career area. (For summer employment, keep looking. If you can't find a job, learn a skill such as typing which will make it easier for you in future summers.)

B. Being interviewed:

1. Remember, you have to sell the employer on the idea that you would be an asset to the company.

2. Before the interview, learn something about the firm so that you can speak intelligently with the person interviewing you.

3. Get to the interview fifteen minutes before you are due there.

4. Be neat, clean, and dressed for the occasion. If a job calls for wearing jeans while you work, then they can be worn for the interview. If you are expected to wear business clothes, then wear them to the interview.

5. Look alert and alive, and don't slump.

6. When you meet the person who is interviewing you, make it a point to learn his name. If necessary ask him to spell it.

7. Think before answering any question. Be honest.

8. Have a résumé of your work career with you. This is a listing of every job you have ever held, exactly which firm you worked for, and the dates of your employment. If you never worked, list your courses in school and personal references.

9. Use correct English. You are not speaking to one of your friends.

10. Don't allow yourself to giggle nervously, or bite your nails.

11. Remember the employer is interested only in how well you will do on this job. He doesn't care if you need it.

12. Be ready to show how your training will help you to get ahead on the job you are asking for. Give an impression of confidence.

13. Have a list of three people you can ask to give you references. They may be asked to write letters about you. Check with each person you plan to name to be sure he or she is willing to cooperate with you.

Activities

1. Place several advertisements on the board. Have the class write letters asking for interviews. Then elect a committee which will read the letters and select those people who would be interviewed for the job, based on their letters. Review the correct form, and give the students examples.

2. Divide the class into groups and role play job interviews. Set up the situations from actual want ads in the newspapers. Have the pupils work out interview questions in advance. Instruct one person to interview another, and the rest of the group to observe and criticize the interview.

3. Have the pupils prepare a resume of their backgrounds and experience. Then have them prepare one for a person they know or for a celebrity. Give them a form to keep for their use in the future.

4. Discuss the aspects of job hunting and being interviewed in terms of situations the pupils will encounter. In other words, set up particular circumstances and help the young people to draw up plans of action. Consider looking for summer jobs, and for that first career job.

NINTH GRADE—SEGMENT TWO

The following career clusters are to be covered:

Fine Arts and Humanities
Public Service
Environment
Marketing and Distribution
Marine Science

At the end of this sequence, take time to do a thorough review of all fifteen of the career clusters. You may wish to divide the class into committees, assigning one cluster to each.

This is important in terms of a wrap-up, a termination for all of the work in career development.

You may wish to ask each youngster to do one career survey of the career that interests him or her the most. If this is done, be sure to have the student check the job opportunities in the immediate area, as well as all of the other information called for in the formal career investigation.

11

Career Education in Grades Ten, Eleven, and Twelve

The Career Education Program is ideally a full program beginning in the elementary school and terminating in the twelfth grade. It can, however, be initiated at any point in a student's education. Unfortunately far too many students have never been exposed to career education, and its lack may hamper them throughout their lives. It is in the tenth, eleventh, and twelfth grades that one of the most important aspects of the program is given, namely the teaching of skills in a particular subject area. These skills enable the young person to enter a career with the knowledge of how to perform a particular job when he graduates.

One of the major differences between the Career Education Program and regular high school programs is that in the former every student is encouraged (or required, depending on your standards) to take a career-entry course. This includes those students who plan on going to college and have been taking academic courses as well as those who are in the so-called general course. The reasons for this are readily understandable. Many young people begin college, then drop out and are as untrained, when it comes to offering skills to an employer, as the young people who took the general course.

The courses the high school must offer, if the Career Education Program is adopted, are quite different from those of the regular, so-called academic high school. They would include many offered today by the vocational schools. The term "comprehensive high school" has been adopted to describe the situation in which vocational and academic courses are both offered. Of course, there have

SATURDAY, MAY 26, 1973

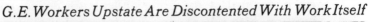

The New York Times

33
L

G.E. Workers Upstate Are Discontented With Work Itself

Vernon Tongue, lathe operator, at work with Ronald McMorris, left, apprentice, at Schenectady. Mr. Tongue would like to retire. His aide wants to get ahead.

Dawn Singleton, an operator for G.E. in Hudson Falls, hopes to work in a nursing home.

By PHILIP SHABECOFF
Special to The New York Times

SCHENECTADY, N.Y., May 25—Workers at the General Electric Company's upstate New York plants are brimming with discontent as their old wage contract expires.

It is not that they are unhappy with the company or their unions, and few seem angry to the point of rebellion. It is rather discontent with the condition of work itself.

According to dozens of workers interviewed at two G.E. plants, their work is not particularly oppressive physically but it is hard enough to send them home exhausted every night.

The routine is not overly demanding, but neither is it particularly interesting. The pay is not unduly depressed, but neither is it adequate in a time of rising prices.

They work for the General Electric Company not because that is their ambition but because that is where the work happens to be—it is a job.

One of the arresting things about these men and women is that so many of them have something else they would rather be doing.

Ryan Henry, for example, a red-bearded, slightly sardonic young man, works as a milling machine operator at General Electric's "mother plant" here but would much rather race stock cars.

"It costs thousands of dollars to build a competitive car," he explained to a visitor encountered at the local offices of the International Union of Electrical Workers just outside the plant gates. "So I work while."

Rose Henderson and her twin sister, Ruth Willard, have been working side by side for 25 years at G.E.'s capacitator plant in Hudson Falls, an hour's drive north of here. They spend most of their spare time raising and selling vegetables and both of them said—with feeling—that if they had their choice they would be farmers just as their parents had been.

"You can't make a living from a small farm anymore," said Miss Henderson, a dry, sprightly woman. "A lot of people working right here at G.E. are farmers who couldn't make a go of it. But you can get used to factory work after a while."

There was no militancy evident among the workers at either plant. They recall with pain the 100-day strike against G.E. three years ago. But virtually without exception they said they were ready to go on strike again if summoned.

At the moment such a summons does not seem imminent. The negotiations, which will affect some 166,000 hourly workers in some 160 General Electric plants around the country, may not be successfully concluded before the deadline

Continued on Page 62, Column 5

:, SATURDAY, MAY 26, 1973

G.E. Workers Feel Discontented With Work Itself

Continued From Page 33

tomorrow. But there seems to be no urge to rush to the picket lines among the 11 unions involved in the bargaining.

The two biggest unions, the International Union of Electrical Workers and the United Electrical Workers Union, have not called general board meetings to discuss further action until the middle of next week.

One of the largest G.E. factories in Schenectady is the turbine and generator plant. A quarter of a mile long, covering 23 acres, it is cavernous, murky, filled with screeching, pounding noises, flickering red and yellow lights and thick, faintly tainted air. Giant 200-ton steel turbine housings squat massively on the floor of the building like bulbous, ancient sea beasts.

Operating one of the big lathes in the turbine plant were Vernon Tongue, who has been with General Electric for 33 years, and Ronald McMorris, a 26-year-old apprentice. Working from blueprints they were shaping a huge rotor to drive a turbine.

"It's not difficult physically but it is very trying mentally," said Mr. Tongue, a small wiry, voluble man. Pointing to the big machine he operated he explained: "You have to get tolerances down to thousandths of an inch. You have to be cautious, very cautious, because it can cost a lot of money if you make a mistake."

Mr. Tongue makes about $15,000 a year with overtime

and finds the work and the company "not too bad." But he would rather be doing something less, to wit, living in retirement.

"We need an early retirement provision in the contract—30 years and out or something like that," he said after turning off his machine to talk. "If you've spent your whole life in a factory, 65 is too late to retire. It ought to be 60 or 62 years when they let you retire so you have some life left to enjoy."

"What's wrong with the factory? Well, listen right now." A thin but very high pitched whine filled the big plant. "Maybe that doesn't hurt your ears but if you hear it day in and day out it bothers you," he said. "This air is polluted. By the end of the day its pretty stale. And you don't see the sunlight from the time you come to work till the time you leave."

Wants to Get Ahead

"I've done my work," Mr. Tongue said. "People who work in factories should be entitled to some rewards. Let somebody else take over. Just give a better pension."

Mr. Tongue says he just does not understand the "attitude" of young workers today. "They don't seem to care at all about the future," he observed. "They want things right now and if they don't get what they want they just pick up and leave their jobs. This wasn't the way we were brought up."

Mr. McMorris, the young

apprentice who works with him, hardly seems to match Mr. Tongue's image of a young worker. After putting in an eight-hour day at the lathe, Mr. McMorris goes to school for about three hours as part of his apprenticeship program. Then he has to face an hour and a half of homework.

Blond, bespectacled and well-spoken, Mr. McMorris finds the work at G.E. "kind of rough." Sometimes it is monotonous, he explained, and at the end of his long day he is often exhausted. He is bothered by the stale air and by the fact that he cannot see the sun.

"But it is very important at this point in my life to do what I have to do so that I can get ahead," he said. "I want to stay here at G.E. and advance myself so that I can provide security for my family."

Davis Willingham, who has been with G.E. for 30 years, says that his work as a chipper and grinder on the big turbines is very physical and tiring. But he likes it, he said, "because it beats walking the streets trying to find something to do."

But as Mr. Willingham told it, his troubles begin when he looks at his pay check. He makes something over $4 an hour but "with five kids and with food prices what they are I can just barely make ends meet. In fact without overtime I wouldn't be able to do it."

Mr. Willingham hopes the International Union of Electrical Workers will be able to win a sizable wage increase for him but is not sanguine. "It's hard to fight G.E. and the Government, too. They got us right in the middle."

The Hudson Falls plant is smaller and more airy, and is set in a soft rural landscape.

However, the workers in Hudson Falls are, if anything, even more edgy than their colleagues in Schenectady. G. E. employees there are members of the United Electrical Workers Union (the I.U.E. and the U.E. split over politics after World War II) and appear to be slightly more militant.

George Crosier, who makes $3.60 an hour as a punch press operator, is 34 years old and, like many workers at the G.E. plants, looks considerably older than his age. A former union shop steward, Mr. Crosier was ready with a litany of complaints when questioned by a visitor.

"No, I don't like this work. Not really. There's a lot of

heavy lifting. The pay is low considering the tolerance we have to work to. We got problems with supervisors who hired you all day long. Whatever you do is wrong. The cost of living escalator doesn't near cover what's happening to the price of meat and potatoes. I tell you, this G.E. is a terrible company. They never get enough of you. They always want more.

Not all of the Hudson Falls workers are dissatisfied. Manfred Johnston, a 59-year-old assembler of induction heaters, works as part of a team and finds his work "interesting and challenging." G.E. is a good company to work for, he feels, and as for going out on strike—"I don't know as I'd really want to."

But in general, the G.E. plants were alive with worker discontent.

Job 'Terribly Boring'

Dawn Singleton, a diminutive blonde of 19, found her job as an assembly bench operator "terribly boring" and hoped to go back someday to work in a nursing home.

Tony Barber, a 42-year-old repair worker, liked his work when he started 17 years ago but now finds it dull, underpaid and unhealthy. "I'd really like to be a plumber—but it's too late for me."

Bernie Loenka, a metalizer who make $148 a week and takes home $97 of that, told a visitor to the local union office that he has to work at a second job as a bartender in order to support his family, which includes four children. "Do you know," he said, "that on what I take home from G.E. I would be eligible for food stamps?"

Priscilla Roof, who operates two winding machines, wears blue jeans and has a madonna face, thinks General Electric practices discrimination against women. "They pay the same for women as men in the same jobs all right, but they just dont' upgrade women. It's starting to change but not fast enough."

Richard White, a 30-year-old machine operator works at G.E. because "it's a job."

To Mike McDowell, a 24-year-old Vietnam veteran working as a service operator, "It's a job."

Mr. Dwyer Burns, who is 61 and makes racks for electrical equipment, says that the work isn't too bad but dislikes the fact that his supervisors "push, push, push all the time."

But, he explained, "It's a job."

been business subjects in high schools for a long time, as there have been home economics and industrial arts courses. However, the latter were not aimed at preparing students for employment. With career education, high school administrators are being asked to change their curricula to include work which was heretofore only given in the vocational schools, technical institutes or colleges. Ideally, courses should be offered in each of the fifteen cluster areas. To be practical, these courses would have to be in areas in which there are job opportunities in your community.

Today there are thousands of vocational programs being given in high schools throughout the United States. The ones we have chosen to include are here because they illustrate new or different approaches to the requirements of career education. While these schools or systems may offer a huge variety of courses, only one or two will be mentioned in these pages. This in no way implies a description of the full offerings of any school or system. We are indebted to the many educators who supplied us with information about their programs. In the event that the reader is interested, he or she is advised to communicate with the school district superintendent or the high school principal for further information. Let us begin, however, with those students entering high school who have never had any courses in career education.

THE NEED TO BEGIN AT THE BEGINNING

There are certain procedures we feel you should follow if your students have never had previous work in career education.

The number of students who have never been involved in a study of careers, occupations or the like is truly astounding. The Career Education Program is a nationwide attempt to remedy this. However, even if they come to you in the ninth or tenth grade, they need this introductory material. They need it badly. There are thousands of different careers open to them, yet there are many of which they are completely ignorant. The need for introductory career education cannot be shown more clearly than by this article, which appeared in *The New York Times* of May 26, 1973. Career choice is one of the areas we have virtually ignored in our educational system, yet one which is badly needed.

How can this lack be made up? We suggest the one-year course, using the curriculum outlined in this book but taught, of course, at the intellectual level of the students. The questionnaires included offer material for self-exploration, which may be used to great advantage with even slower learners.

The curriculum lends itself to a year's work, which, we believe, is a minimum amount of time to spend on this very critical area. Time allotments can be shifted to suit the particular class. If, for example, the course is being given to a group which has few students aiming to go on for posthigh school education, the stress would be on job opportunities for the high school graduate. Technical careers should be emphasized, however, because many of these require only two, rather than four years of college.

THE SELECTION OF A SKILLS COURSE
FROM A CLUSTER AREA

Again, speaking ideally, if a high school were to adopt a full Career Education Program, it would be able to offer to its students a choice of courses preparing for entry-level jobs in any of the fifteen cluster areas. Practically, one must realize we are far away from this ideal. However, if we throw up our hands and give up, we rob our children of a great deal. It is infinitely better to begin by offering one or two career-entry courses, and increase the number and variety year by year.

There is no question but that opportunities for career-oriented high school education are far greater in large cities than in smaller communities. (This was one of the situations Dr. Conant pointed out in 1959 in *The American High School Today*.) As an example, there are 42,000 students (learning eighty trades) in the New York City high schools. It is to remedy this lack in smaller school systems that career education has come into being—and that career-oriented courses are being added to the comprehensive high school curricula all over the country.

Your first consideration must be in terms of the requirements of your community. What courses are needed? Where are there job opportunities? This information can point out the direction in which to proceed.

The following sections are composed of a variety of career-entry offerings. Some are in individual high schools, whereas others are to be found in schools in central locations serving students from a number of high schools. All, however, are attempts to meet specific needs, as you will see when you read about them.

THE STATE OF WASHINGTON
AND THE FISHING INDUSTRY

Sea Resources, Inc., is a program originated and operated by the Ocean Beach School District located in Ilwaco, Washington. Ilwaco is located in Pacific county at the mouth of the Columbia River. The industries of the county are fishing and logging-wood products. The tourist industry also contributes to the county's economy, but this is directly related to sport fishing. Pacific county ranks twenty-seventh of thirty-nine counties with a population of 15,796. The Ilwaco High School has 472 students enrolled in grades nine through twelve. The placement of students from the "Commercial and Tourist Fishing" program has been twelve out of fifteen enrollees. Considering the financial and demographic conditions of the area, this program is very successful.

The material that follows is from a report on Sea Resources published with funds supplied by the Economic Development Administration. This venture was the result of cooperation between the Federal governmental agencies, the local industries, and the local schools.

Sea Resources, Inc. was formed to fund and operate an otherwise impossible sea and fisheries training program in this area. The reasons for the program can be summarized as follows: A. To train local students, utilize their home backgrounds, area background, terrain, marine environment, boats, gear and skills; to provide jobs at home; and to help general welfare and the cause of Fisheries and Oceanography. B. To provide introductory skills to noncollege-bound students and intellectual stimulus to the college-bound. C. To provide students with a "head start" in Fisheries for further training. D. To help the local situation which is very much dependent on Fisheries for tourist trade in its various aspects.

Laurence Prest, first course instructor, gave an interesting account of that course, which is summarized here. The course ran for one-half year, during the spring semester. Sixteen students were enrolled for a three-hour period each afternoon. Emphasis was on fisheries training to enable a student to acquire skills that would get him a summer job during the coming fishing season. Areas covered in classroom work, held at the Chinook Fire Hall, included knots, splicing rope and cable, use and care of rope, crab pot construction and repair, navigation, navigation by dead reckoning, bearings, beacons, loran, and soundings.

In good weather outside activity was carried on. Work was done on hatchery building, nursery channel, ponds, stream diversion, trapping of fish, beaver control, boat maintenance, and operation. Students were taken on commercial crab fishing trips over the Columbia River Bar, usually a trip of five or six hours. There the student was allowed to participate and on the trip he was taught by the boat captain and deckhand. Each student had a number of trips. Local boat captains were very cooperative in taking the students. Students were taken for instruction on a commercial charter boat furnished by Lee Timmen, Jr. Included in this section of work were: boat handling, navigation, trolling, rigging commercial and sport fishing gear, engine maintenance, hull repair, maintenance, and seamanship.

WSCOE

Field trips to research stations and commercial processing plants were taken during the course and lectures were given by Bureau of Fisheries speakers, prominent in national and northwest fisheries.

At the conclusion of the course, effort was made to place all students in fisheries work. Seven found employment on fishing and charter boats, two in the oyster industry, one with the Bureau of Commercial Fisheries, one as a mechanic and three are in non-fisheries work. Five of these are still year-round fishermen, one is a fish buyer and one is a cannery worker. In 1971, six are in cannery work, three are trolling and three gillnetting, and we expect more to get jobs as the season progresses and school ends. The students all felt that their course training had helped them secure work and interested them in fisheries as a career.

THE CAREER DEVELOPMENT CENTER IN DALLAS

The following description of the Skyline Center for Career Development illustrates the manner in which career education needs are being met through a central school and campus. Please note that funding is being done by the Independent School District of Dallas.

The program is an extensive one, but, we must point out, it falls short of the idealized goal of career education since every young person does not receive some form of career training. However, Skyline Center might well serve as a prototype for comprehensive high schools which would be able to do a very adequate job with career education.

The Skyline Center is located on an eighty-acre campus. The building itself covers fourteen acres. Skyline Center is a multipurpose facility intended to provide maximum educational opportunity to the citizens of the Dallas Independent School District.

Skyline High School

At the core of Skyline Center is Skyline High School. As a regular comprehensive high school it offers the basic curriculum of other Dallas schools, has regular activities such as football and student government, and has set student assignment boundaries. The head of the school is the principal.

Career Development Center

The Career Development Center is an extension of all Dallas high schools. Students may attend the center on a part-time basis to take daily three hour blocks of Career Education Programs or may transfer to the center full time by becoming a Skyline High School student. A shuttle bus service from each Dallas high school is provided by the district free of charge to students attending the Career Development Center.

Center for Community Services

As an extension of the adult education program of the Dallas Independent School District, the Community Service component operates an extensive day and evening program at Skyline Center. This program includes both credit and noncredit courses and utilizes the modern facilities of the Center.

The CDC Commitment to Career Education

Skyline Career Development Center represents a firm commitment by the Dallas Independent School District to provide students with education beyond the ordinary. The center's CDC programs are intended to enable each student to maintain a balance of academic and career education. The curriculum is designed to provide each CDC student with (1) a high school diploma, (2) the preparation to enter college or technical school, and (3) career skills to be used for future employment or to put the student a step ahead in advanced education.

The CDC Cluster Concept

Skyline Career Development Center is organized into career clusters. Each cluster encompasses several families of careers. These families are in turn made up of many specific career options. In most cases a student spends three hours daily working within a career cluster. His needs and his specific career interest determine his individual course of study and how much time he spends on individual tasks.

Within a three-hour block of career cluster time a student may participate in several varied experiences. He may work with small or large groups; he may do independent study; he may work on a specific project; or, perhaps, he might take a field trip to investigate a career option. At Skyline a student's individual needs and interests dictate his assignments.

Student Body

The student body of Skyline Center is composed of four types of students: (1) those who live within the Skyline High School attendance zones, (2) those who transfer to Skyline High School as full-time students in order to take advantage of Career Development courses, (3) those who attend the Career Development Center on a part-time basis and remain enrolled at their local school, and (4) adults or other part-time students who enroll in the Community Service Program.

Career Development Center Clusters

Advanced English, Journalism
Advanced Mathematics
Advanced Science
Architectural Careers
Aviation Technology
Business and Management Careers
Child Related Professions
Computer Technology
Cosmetology
Electronic Sciences
Food Services and Management
Graphics Communication
Horticulture

Interior Design
Man and His Environment
Medical and Dental Careers
Performing Arts
Photographic Arts
Television Arts
Transportation Services
Visual Arts
World Languages
World of Construction
World of Environmental
   Control Systems
World of Fashion
World of Manufacturing

Grades, attendance records, general success in the academic school programs, and a good discipline record serve as indications of success in the Career Development Center.

PARMA, OHIO'S TELEVISION PRODUCTION AND BROADCASTING

In Parma, Ohio, the program offered to Normandy High School students is truly exceptional. This is a two-year Television Production and Broadcasting program which offers students a unique opportunity that is rarely equaled anywhere. The three-hour class provides young people with daily professional training and experience in various television production techniques, utilizing the excellent facilities of the Parma Instructional Television Service as a laboratory.

Students in the course are involved in the various production activities for the ITV programs broadcast over the TV station owned by the school board. In this way, students gain realistic experience in a professional atmosphere. The areas of study include: photography and film development, graphics and titles, art work, stage design and construction, studio lighting, camera operation, and many other related and essential studio production techniques.

Through exercises and student-prepared activities, wider experiences are gained in such skills as script writing, producing and directing, audio, video, switching, and announcing. In addition, there are discussions of the basic nature of the television industry focusing on TV history, TV operations, programming practices, commercials, ratings, and current broadcasting issues.

Second year students in the program gain greater skill and sophistication in all of the creative and technical areas while pursuing specialization and independent study of their own interest. They also serve as production aids and help in teaching basic skills. Some internship and workshop programs are available through the Pace Foundation, various stations, and the Cleveland Chapter of the National Association of Television Arts and Sciences. Those wishing to apply for TV Production are asked to have a good background in some of the following areas: stagecraft, AVA, photography, art, graphics, music, and dramatics. They should also be mature indi-

Parma Public Schools, Parma, Ohio

viduals who are self-motivated, outgoing, creative, dependable, hard-working and, above all, very interested in the field of television.

The course is specifically designed to suit the needs and interests of students planning a career in some aspect of television production. There are several allied occupational areas that students enter as a result of the experience and training gained in this program. While some graduates continue studying broadcasting in college, others seek employment after graduation. Students are prepared for entry-level jobs as cameramen, stagehands, production assistants, etc. in smaller television markets, cable TV outlets, instructional television operations, and some aspects of radio. It must be noted, however, that the TV industry is highly competitive and jobs are not easily found. Securing employment and achieving success in this exciting and creative field are very difficult, but well worth the struggle.

NEW YORK'S HAAREN HIGH SCHOOL MINI-SCHOOLS

The information that follows is particularly important in terms of selecting courses (at Haaren they are referred to as Mini-Schools). These are courses that appeal to inner-city residents, and which are geared to them. Thus their work in school will help the young adults to develop skills that almost insure their employability.

The First National City Bank of New York City, advertises:

The "mini-school news," published by the New York Urban Coalition has a headline "Big business is a big help."

Haaren is growing up. And it's had a lot of help. From the New York Urban Coalition which fostered Haaren's new baby (the mini-school) and from the business community, which is nurturing it.

Haaren couldn't go it alone. Of course, it never came to that. The Urban Coalition was there and business responded. Experts from corporations *volunteered* their time, manpower, energy, equipment and money to get Haaren off and running by leaving it basically free to just carry on.

And it is.

Oh, things aren't perfect. But it would be hard to argue that Haaren's mini-schools aren't moving in the right direction.

Look at who is or was involved: American Airlines, Atlantic Richfield, Celanese, Coalition-JOBS, Con Edison, First National City Bank, General Electric, General Motors, McGraw Hill, Mobil, New York Art Directors Club, New York Transit Authority, New York Telephone, Port Authority of New York, Seagrams, Standard Oil of New Jersey, Union Carbide and United Airlines.

We're helping Haaren High turn drop-outs into stay-ins. You can help, too.

Average class attendance —
May, 1971

Manhattan's Haaren High School has been converted from a single school of over 2,500 students into twelve autonomous educational units averaging 150 to 200 students and six teachers each.

A complex of twelve mini-schools.

The objective is for each mini-school to become a dramatically more exciting learning and teaching environment, each with a different theme and curriculum geared to the students' real educational needs. And with more student-teacher interaction.

Teachers and staff at Haaren now look forward to each new day of classes. And a lot of students who were on their way to dropping out are now on their way to diplomas.

In fact, during the last six weeks of the school year, a time when attendance used to fall off drastically, the number of absentees was cut in half in several of the mini-schools.

This program was developed by Haaren's teachers, principal and students with the support of the Urban Coalition, the Board of Education and several corporations.

At First National City, we were glad we could help. For over a year, we participated in planning and testing the first mini-

school model with the Urban Coalition. And at the invitation of the principal and faculty, we moved to Haaren, where we helped draw up a new management blueprint so the mini-school idea could be executed with no increase in personnel or materials. And at no extra cost to the taxpayer.

We learned, too, that many of the management techniques we use with our 16,000 New York employees can also be effective in secondary education.

Of course, there's plenty more to do.

As more city high schools convert to mini-schools, they will need help from more city businesses. They will need the kind of organizational and administrative help that businesses can give together with help in rearranging teaching schedules and re-allocating resources.

Average class attendance —
May, 1972

If you are in a position to make recommendations to your firm that it help the mini-school idea become possible elsewhere in the city, you can learn more details by writing to Mr. Louis B. McCagg at the Urban Coalition, 55 Fifth Avenue, New York, N.Y. 10003.

NEW YORK:
WE'RE ALL IN IT TOGETHER.

FIRST NATIONAL CITY BANK

99 PARK AVENUE, NEW YORK, N.Y. 10022 • MEMBER FDIC

First National City Bank of New York

Now, take a peek at what's been done. Haaren now has a video studio for students and teachers because *Celanese* and Open Channel were interested. The Automotive Mini-School now has all kinds of equipment because *Exxon* was interested. The Aviation Mini-School has a real airplane in the basement of the school.

The Haaren curriculum includes a series of mini-schools:

1. A Correlated Curriculum Mini-School offering a four-year program leading toward specific careers in drafting, electronics and transportation.

2. An Automotive Mini-School that leans heavily on courses involving the automotive industry, such as auto mechanics, electricity and math (as it relates to the service station industry).

3. The Aviation Mini-School offers courses ranging from flight principles to communication.

4. English as a Second Language Mini-School helps fulfill the needs of the students who want to learn English.

5. The SHAFT Mini-School emphasizes reading and writing improvement; from here the students move on to one of the other Mini-Schools.

6. A Cooperative Mini-School features a work/study program.

7. The Special Education Mini-School is all job oriented. Once a week its students go out to work in a variety of jobs throughout the city.

8. The Senior Mini-School catches eleventh and twelfth grade students who are not college bound and gets them ready for general service examinations.

9. The High School Equivalency Mini-School takes the older student (over seventeen) who wants a diploma, but might otherwise never go back to get it.

10. The Careers Mini-School is exploratory. It's where a student can find his ambitions and move on. There are incentives such as sales representatives or Armed Forces men who speak to the students.

11. The Pre-Technical Electronics Mini-School prepares the electronically oriented student for college level courses of study through the use of video equipment, math, and related areas of study.

12. The College Bound Mini-School does exactly that—prepares the academic student for college.

This is an example of the active cooperation of the business community and the educational institution to meet the needs of everyone concerned.

ON-THE-JOB EXPLORATION AND TRAINING
IN WHITTIER, CALIFORNIA

The Whittier Union High School District offers its students opportunities for paid or nonpaid work experience where the students receive on-the-job training in a field related to school training, past or present.

The Exploratory Work Experience

This program is nonpaying, consisting of on-the-job observation and involvement after school hours. Students may receive credit for it, and any student may participate. Students are thoroughly screened, and assigned to a "trainer" to "explore" for a limited period of time. They are not required to do productive work. They learn, for example, what is required to be a laboratory technician by actually observing and working with one. They are rated by the trainer for dependability, interest and attitude. Students are supervised on the job by school personnel. They may explore accounting, business administration, city administration, cosmetology, dental assisting, dentistry, engineering, law, nursing, physical therapy, and welding.

The Vocational Work Experience

Eleventh and twelfth graders are paid for working a minimum of ten hours during the school week. They must be presently enrolled in a related class or have received vocational training as a job-entry requirement. Students are screened carefully. They work under a trainer who is skilled in the field in such areas as clerk typist, food handler, auto mechanic, machinist, printer, retail clerk, station attendant, draftsman, or upholstery worker. They are supervised on the job, and evaluations are made of their progress. They also earn credits toward their graduation.

The General Work Experience

This program involves paid work experience for eleventh and twlefth grade students who do not work in an area related to their school training. Students are assigned, after screening, to work that will enrich their general school program. In all other respects this is similar to the Vocational Work Experience Program.

The Whittier program illustrates a valid technique for giving

STUDENT EMPLOYMENT STORY

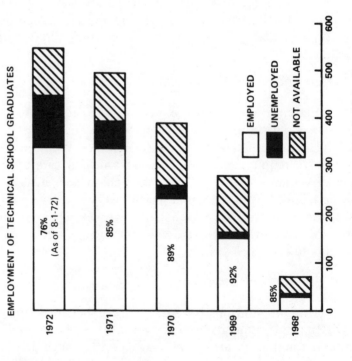

EMPLOYMENT OF TECHNICAL SCHOOL GRADUATES

1972 — 76% (As of 8-1-72)
1971 — 85%
1970 — 89%
1969 — 92%
1968 — 85%

EMPLOYED
UNEMPLOYED
NOT AVAILABLE

St. Louis County Technical Schools

1968 1969 1970 1971

1972
FOLLOW-UP
STUDY OF
VOCATIONAL
STUDENTS

Special School District
State of Missouri
National

68.5%
47.3%
55.5%

Oct., 1970, most recent federal figures available

Special School District of St. Louis County
Oral W. Spurgeon, Superintendent

North Tech
South Tech

young people entry-level skills and/or a time to explore the career area in which they are interested—so they know if they wish to continue in it, seek further training, or find an altogether new area.

SPECIAL SCHOOL DISTRICT
OF ST. LOUIS COUNTY, MISSOURI

The St. Louis County Technical School programs have been developed to serve their community and the communities surrounding it by training young people in skill areas for which there are distinct needs, and in which there are job openings.

The graph that follows illustrates the success the entire curriculum has had:

The Special School District of St. Louis County sees itself as having two separate and distinct responsibilities. One of these is Special Education (for the handicapped). The second is Vocational-Technical Education for noncollege-bound students who wish to enter a program that prepares them for entry as advanced learners into the businesses and industries of the area.

The information brochure put out by the St. Louis County Technical Schools is a truly exceptional one. We suggest you write to Oral W. Spurgeon, Superintendent, Special School District of St. Louis County, Central Office, 9820 Manchester Road, Rock Hill, Mo. 63119 for a copy. It is one of the very best pieces of motivational material we have ever seen—well worth using as a prototype. It lists a great variety of programs.

The Ornamental Horticulture is one we found worthy of mention. The course provides organized subject matter and practical experiences in the production, marketing, and servicing of all types of horticultural plants and products. In addition, the instruction emphasizes knowledge important to establishing, maintaining, and managing ornamental horticulture enterprises. Related science and math are required, and a course in industrial communications is included.

Much of the work is performed either in greenhouses or outdoors working with flowering plants, trees, shrubs, and turf. Even though there is still much hand labor in horticulture, emphasis is being placed on power equipment such as rototillers and tractors.

The course content includes an introduction to horticulture; plant science; soil science; greenhouse operation and management; landscaping, design, construction, and maintenance; nursery operation and management; growing, arranging and selling flowers and plants; and turf management.

In September 1973, a number of new programs were being offered. These include Diesel Truck Mechanic, Child Care Assistant, Air Frame and Power Mechanics, and Cosmetology.

The Technical Schools also serve the community by offering adult evening classes in a great variety of skill areas.

One of the slogans used is "Every teacher a tradesman" in each program offered. Advisory committees are the means of communication. They enable educators and industry to work together for training programs most suitable for the community.

THE TRI-COUNTY JOINT VOCATIONAL HIGH SCHOOL OF NELSONVILLE, OHIO

The philosophy and purposes, as they are stated by the administration of the school, are as follows:

> The establishment of a joint vocational-technical training center is based on the precept that the "area concept" is the most realistic method in a basically rural sector, such as Southeastern Ohio, to provide vocational-technical training. Individual districts cannot afford this type of facility but by pooling resources, it can be made available to serve the needs of the entire area.
>
> The doors of the school shall be open to "anyone" who sincerely wants, needs, and can profit from vocational instruction. High school students and out-of-school people will be training and learning side by side in "ungraded" classes to provide a "person-centered" approach.
>
> A broad spectrum of program offerings is available, including those which will challenge the high ability person to optimum achievement and those which will stimulate and motivate the slow learner to succeed.
>
> Programs will be constantly up-dated to avoid obsolescence and will be in keeping with the occupational opportunities prevailing in the world of work. In view of the rapid pace of technological change, it becomes more and more important to have the training opportunity for entry into and retention of gainful employment in today's labor market.
>
> The facilities of the school represent a significant investment of local, state, and federal funds. Multiple use of facilities for regular and special programs and a wide variety of residual services to participating schools is planned to realize optimum returns on this investment. In full operation, the school will be in use 12 months per year.

An example of a course needed by the members of the community is Agricultural Equipment and Mechanics:

Agriculture Equipment and Mechanics

Many occupational opportunities exist in the agricultural machinery services. As farms become larger and methods of production become more technical in nature, a wider variety of services will be required from agricultural machinery dealerships. The need for competent employees in the agricultural machinery service occupation is further exemplified by the interest which has developed on the part of employers in hiring competent people to fill positions in the service occupations.

The purpose of this program is to develop the degree of competencies needed for entry and advancement in the service occupations in agricultural machinery and equipment dealerships. The instructional and training program would cover the maintenance and repair of field machinery and other agricultural equipment.

Law Enforcement Program

This Law Enforcement Training Program is designed to provide enough skill aptitude and related knowledge for a student to enter law enforcement at the patrolman level, private enterprise as a security agent, or other law enforcement related agencies at their starting level.

The high school course includes Math, Administration of Justice, History of Law Enforcement, Law Enforcement, Federal, State, County, City, Village, Defensive Tactics, Emergencey Victim Care, Business and Industrial Security, Report Writing, Crimes and Elements of the Law, Ethics and Canons of Law Enforcement, Techniques of Law Enforcement Photography, Data Processing as Applied to Law Enforcement, Sciences and Laboratory Used in Law Enforcement and Patrolling and Driving Techniques Used in Law Enforcement.

This program gives excellent training for those persons interested in entering the Law Enforcement Technology. Employment opportunities are excellent. Our society is demanding more security and safety in the pursuit of living.

AVIATION—THE AUGUST MARTIN HIGH SCHOOL, QUEENS, N.Y.

The August Martin High School in the borough of Queens, New York City, is a comprehensive high school with specific curriculum emphasis on air transport industry programs to fulfill the needs of the John F. Kennedy International Airport, located about a mile away. There is emphasis, too, on the entire aerospace industry.

There are many educational innovations, such as the following:

1. Every student has a nine-period day.

2. The school year is based on four cycles (terms) instead of the traditional two.

3. Modular scheduling techniques are used constantly.

4. Every student has a daily period of independent study.

5. Airport facilities are utilized for special training.

6. The school operates a double summer session of three and one-half weeks each.

7. Curriculum innovations include:
   Basic and Advanced Meteorology
   Basic and Advanced Navigation
   Airport and Airline Management
   Pre-Stewardess Orientation
   Flight Planning and Instruction
   Federal Aviation Laws and Regulations (including Air Traffic Control)
   Avionics (electronic communications)
   Travel and Tourism
   Basic and Aerial Photography

8. As far as possible, the classroom instruction in the professional electives will be supplemented by field trips and off-campus laboratory work at airport facilities.

Students whose interests lean toward a technology education in a four-year or community college will have the opportunity to select a curriculum pattern in Aerospace Design Technology or Aerospace Medical Technology.

The projected program of study in aerospace design technology includes Mathematics, Phsyics, and Basic Engineering Drawing in the eleventh year, followed by Manufacturing Processes, Materials Testing, and Mechanical Design and/or Architectural Design in the twelfth year.

The projected program of study in Aerospace Medical Technology includes Mathematics, Chemistry, and Medical Techniques Laboratory work in the eleventh year, followed by Medical Therapy, Patient Care, Medical Office Practices, and Medical Typing in the twelfth year.

Pupils desiring occupational training will be able to elect from

High schoolers skipping classes for internship

By RAYMOND A. WITTEK

Twenty-five Staten Island high school students are regularly skipping classes.

But they needn't look over their shoulders to see if a truant officer is after them.

The students don't show up for attendance at school. Instead they report for "work" four days a week at a governmental agency, civic organization or private business, and put in a 9-to-5 work day.

The students are participating in an executive internship program jointly sponsored by the Board of Education and the Office of Educational Development of the U.S. Human Resources Administration.

One of the program's goals seems to be taken from a page in a Ralph Nader study. According to Miss Marguerite Greenfield, HRA borough director for the program, the interns are encouraged to "look critically at the agency" to which they are assigned. But she adds this is done in an attempt to develop the students' "critical thinking and analytical skills."

Other goals of the program, she said, are intended to develop the interns' skills, provide them with an insight into careers and to participate in community activities.

The program has been confined so far to New York City, although other cities have expressed an interest in it. Since its inception in the fall of 1971, the program has had 400 interns. However, Miss Greenfield said she hopes to have 500 enrolled in it this spring. On Staten Island, she hopes to double the present number to 50.

For two seniors at New Dorp High School, the program has added an important new dimension to their final year, turning it from what they regarded as a minus to a plus.

"It has given real meaning to our senior year," said one of them, Daniel Bianchini of 130 Lamport Blvd., South Beach. "Ordinarily you feel you can coast in your senior year."

But Bianchini and his classmate, Philip Bofa of 169 McFarland Ave., also South Beach, feel that the intern program has altered this attitude, turning their senior year into a meaningful, practical experience.

The program, however, isn't restricted to seniors, being open also to juniors.

In a capsule, the program transfers students from the classroom to the world of government and business. The students spend one semester in the program. One day each week the interns spend attending a seminar, at which they discuss what they have been doing, decide on reading material to implement their practical experience and other matters.

FULL CREDIT

Miss Greenfield said the students get full credit for all their normal school subjects while working as interns. They also are given the option to prepare for Regents examinations, and even if they fail these tests they still receive their regular credits. In addition, the interns are encouraged to pursue independant studies to keep up with the courses they would be taking if in class.

The interns also receive a bonus, as far as their college applications go. Miss Greenfield said the HRA sends colleges descriptions of the intern programs, in addition to a letter of recommendation on behalf of the intern applicant to the school of his choice. She said that 96 to 97 per cent of all interns have been accepted by colleges.

Not all public high schools on the Island are taking part in the program. At present, the participating schools are Port Richmond, Wagner and Tottenville, in addition to New Dorp. Other schools have declined to take part for a variety of reasons, Miss Greenfield said.

Grades are not necessarily a factor in selecting a student for the program, she said, although the student's school has to recommend him. The chief requirements are that the student is "capable of assuming a mature staff role" and has qualities of "leadership, responsibility and maturity," Miss Greenfield said.

To get the program's message across to both the student and "employers" — the students receive no remuneration — two teachers carry out a recruiting program on the Island. They are Ralph Thompson and Jon Schein. They work out of the HRA office at 150 Church St., Manhattan.

Bianchini and Bofa are among three interns assigned to the district attorney's office. Others, however, are working for other govermental agencies nursing homes, colleges, department stores, courts and a select few private businesses.

The program seeks to encourage students to "explore the way agencies in their community serve ther needs," Miss Greenfield said.

The interns are assigned to a wide variety of chores.

The district attorney's office, for example, assigns them clerical tasks and has them sit as observers in criminal proceedings where they may also be called upon to be messengers, calling witnesses and so on.

Assistant District Attorney Thomas F. Lloyd, who has been instrumental in having his office cooperate in the program, looked upon the program as an opportunity to get needed help, in addition to benefitting the student in both a short-range and long-range view.

"Everybody is abusing the criminal justice system from the outside," he said. "The interns can see from the inside what we're doing, perhaps even some good. Even if they don't go into law, they'll remember for the remainder of their lives what we're trying to do."

As far as the district attorney's office goes, Lloyd said it is trying to impart on the students the concept: "We're all people living in the same community."

Staten Island Advance, March 11, 1973

among Ground Support Vehicle Mechanics, Airport Servicing, and Passenger Servicing.

The success of a career-oriented program may depend on many factors. Certainly adequate facilities are extremely important. The August Martin High School is in the process of developing these facilities. Noteworthy, too, are other innovations, such as the nine-period day, and the four-cycle year. These may be adopted for any type of curriculum—again with the purpose of meeting the needs of the students.

THE HIGH SCHOOL INTERNSHIP PROGRAM

The new program that follows is devoted in part to training our youth to work for the nation's largest employers, the Federal, state and city governments. It considers areas that have rarely been discussed or studied in school, and serves as an excellent introduction for young people to this type of career.

LOS ANGELES CAREER ADVISEMENT

In Los Angeles, California, the Division of Career and Continuing Education introduced a new approach in guidance services for career education in September 1971. This new approach is provided through the position of the Regional Occupational Programs (ROP) Career Adviser.

With the increase in career education programs to meet the needs of pupils, it became apparent that career guidance services to high school pupils needed improvement and expansion. While every person on the school staff is responsible for guidance services to pupils, the assumption often has been that someone else was providing the service. In reality, the guidance program was not being fully implemented. The intent of assigning a career advisor was to place specific responsibility for career guidance activities with a person who was part of the school counseling team.

The ROP Career Advisor assists high school pupils with educational and occupational guidance, programming, transportation, and follow-up as it concerns Regional Occupational Programs and Centers in the Los Angeles Unified School District.

The advisors are part of the counseling office staff at the high school and are under the direction of the head counselor. Career Education Instructional Specialists at the four Field Service Centers provide coordination of the advisors' activities in their respective areas. A consultant, at the Division Office, coordinates the program districtwide.

Implementation

Assignments. Thirty-two career advisors served the forty-nine high schools and seven opportunity high schools located throughout the 750-square mile area of the Los Angeles Unified School District. Fifteen advisors were each assigned to one school; each of the other seventeen served two or more schools.

Program Enrollment. The advisor is responsible for programming pupils into the various Regional Occupational Programs at the high school or business and industry site and the Young Adult Program at the Adult Regional Occupational Centers.

Prior to assuming responsibilities at the high school, the ROP Career Advisor participated in an in-service education program. During the school year, fourteen four-hour sessions were conducted at various sites that included:

1. regional occupational centers
2. high schools
3. the Los Angeles Chamber of Commerce
4. the Bell Telephone Company
5. the Prudential Insurance Company
6. The Burbank-Lockheed Company
7. the United States Navy and Marine Reserve Training Center
8. the Association of the United States Army provided air transportation for the advisors to view training at Fort Ord in Monterey

A student can choose from almost 100 different kinds of possible job training in certain high schools in Los Angeles. It's the career advisor's task to help him make a choice, and then to implement it. The career advisors are all individuals who have been in business or industry.

The Los Angeles Career Advisement Program is an example of one metropolis's partial solution to the educational problems of the inner city. While no one solution is possible, we believe this program has proved to be very effective. It also illustrates the most productive use of specially trained counselors in a career education program. It is for this reason that we have gone into detail, and have listed all of the various career-oriented offerings.

XEROX LEARNING SYSTEMS

One answer to the problems of schools that cannot afford to offer skills programs comes to us through the technological advances of our era. The Xerox Corporation has developed what it calls Xerox Learning Systems. For years these systems were used for *advanced* learning programs in business, industry, government, and colleges and universities. Now there are four Learning Systems designed for use with high school students. These are in the following areas:

Automotive Technology
Drafting Technology
Climate Control Technology
Electronics Technology

Audio-Visual Presentation

Cassette lessons are linked to a film strip that is activated by the student or instructor as each part of a lesson is learned. The student sees what he hears. The instructor-on-tape tells the student what to observe . . . to perform activities on a simulator or equipment . . . to solve problems—then waits for answers . . . prods for comprehension . . . asks the student to write answers or draw diagrams on a worksheet to confirm understanding. The presentation is carefully structured to progress from the simple to the complex, with constant opportunity for review by the learner. Most units contain 250 or more visuals and two audio-cassettes.

Simulator

The student immediately puts his new-found knowledge to work with a hands-on simulator. He examines what he's learning . . . tries it . . . checks himself every step of the way. The simulator, which illustrates or resembles on-the-job tasks, lets the student interact with the lesson. He must plug in answers or identify diagram components on the simulator display board—or manipulate equipment. The simulator tells him whether he's on the right track . . . warns him if he's wrong . . . encourages him when he's right . . . fixes the information firmly in his mind.

Worksheets

Worksheets are coordinated with film-strip visuals, the tape-instructor's voice, and the simulator demonstration board. The worksheets allow the student to check his grasp of what he's learning *as he learns it*—and to record what he has learned for his own future use, and for the instructor's check-up and progress reports.

The worksheets also define in simple, step-by-step, written form, the terms and concepts that the learner is absorbing by sight, sound, and simulation.

Performance Goals

What does a student know already? How much more skilled will he be after each lesson? What will he have learned after an entire course? These are the questions that the Xerox Occupational Technology performance goals will help you answer. They give you a list of specific achievements that a learner can accomplish with the Occupational Technology courses.

Pretests tell you how much a student knows to begin with, his general level of knowledge and whether he can skip specific units. Posttests tell both you and the student how much he has learned and whether to return to a unit for more knowledge-reinforcement.

The Instructor's Manual

A special manual for each unit makes it easy for your teacher to oversee or conduct the training. It contains instructions, a list of performance goals, a copy of the entire film-strip script, and the accompanying visuals. Correct answers are given on copies of worksheets and pre- and posttests.

The preceding description was supplied by Xerox, as was the following, when we inquired about price.

> A 10 unit installation with a one learner position would average about $3,500. Ten learner positions with enough material to keep all positions in use in an individualized classroom would cost around $10,000. This amount would provide multiple copies of some units, especially those that are in prerequisite chains.

Of course, this is the initial expenditure.

We feel this type of program makes it possible for many schools to offer technical training which they could otherwise not do, and it is for this reason we have included this information in these pages.

We have been advised that the Lively Vocational-Technical School in Tallahassee, Florida has installed twenty-two units (automotive electronics and climate control—with five learner positions).

There are thirteen Xerox Learning Systems offices across the country. If you are interested, contact this office for further information:

Xerox Learning Systems
Occupational Technology Series
1200 High Ridge Road
Stamford, Conn. 06905

Summary

The Career Education Program reaches its culmination, ideally, in grades ten, eleven, and twelve, when each student is taught skills that will prepare him for a particular vocation. In the event that he goes on for further education, it is possible he may never utilize these skills or he may use them for summer jobs. However, should he drop out of college, he will have them to fall back upon. Other students, not college bound, will be assured of having skills that they may utilize to earn a living.

Before selecting a career area, the student should have been presented with an overall view of occupations and should have been helped to assess his or her own capabilities. If this is done as it should be, from the first grade on, then the student is ready to select a program based on his knowledge. If he or she was not offered this information, then it should be offered even in grades ten, eleven or twelve.

In the high school years, it is incumbent upon us as educators to offer to our youth courses of practical value to them. This will enable them to choose skills programs that will equip them for careers. These programs should take into consideration the needs of both the youth and of the community in which they reside. What can possibly be the point of offering courses when there are few, if any, jobs available? On the other hand, if we do train them for specific areas where we know there is a need for trained personnel, we help both the young person and the community in which he lives.

We have selected ten programs to illustrate this concept. They are in different schools, in various parts of the country. They have one thing in common, however; they are geared to specific occupations, and lead to specific jobs. Should the students elect to go on to college, they can easily do so. In many cases the schools are affiliated in one way or another with local colleges. But, should the students desire to enter the labor force, they have marketable skills that will enable them to begin to work almost immediately in occupations that pay considerably more than the minimum wage, and that have chances for advancement. Information is included, too, regarding commercially available Learning Systems which enable schools to offer technical education through electronic media.

The specific courses and programs are included in these pages to supply you with ideas—so that you may figure out programs that will suit your students and serve your community. Some of these programs began modestly. Others were entire school system efforts, but, nevertheless, all have the manpower needs of the community and the individual student (his vocational and educational future) as the basis for their development.

As we move toward comprehensive high schools, which include in their curricula vocational training for every student as well as college preparation for those who want it, we come closer to full employment through training, and toward a fuller realization of each individual's potential.

APPENDICES

Appendix A

SOURCES OF CAREER INFORMATION
FOR 106 CAREERS

Accountant

National Association of Accountants
505 Park Avenue
New York, N.Y. 10022

Advertising Industry

American Advertising Federation
1225 Connecticut Avenue N.W.
Washington, D.C. 20036

Agent-Insurance

Institute of Life Insurance
277 Park Avenue
New York, N.Y. 10017

Airline Industry

Personnel Officer
Federal Aviation Administration
Eastern Region, Federal Building
J.F. Kennedy Airport
Long Island, N.Y. 11430

Appliance Serviceman

Association of Home Appliance Manufacturers
20 N. Wacker Drive
Chicago, Ill. 60606

Architect

American Institute of Architects
1785 Massachusetts Avenue N.W.
Washington, D.C. 20036

Atomic Energy

U.S. Atomic Energy Commision
Washington, D.C. 20545

Auto Body Repairman

Automotive Service Industry Association
230 N. Michigan Avenue
Chicago, Ill. 60601

Automobile Mechanic

Automotive Service Industry Association
230 N. Michigan Avenue
Chicago, Ill. 60601

Baking Industry

American Bakers Association
1700 Pennsylvania Avenue N.W.
Washington, D.C. 20006

Banking

American Bankers Association
Personnel Administration & Management
Development Committee

	1120 Connecticut Avenue N.W. Washington, D.C. 20036
Barber	National Association of Barber Schools Inc. 750 Third Avenue Huntington, West Virginia 25701
Beautician (Cosmetologist)	National Beauty Career Center 3839 White Plains Road Bronx, New York
Bookbinder	Printing Industry of America 1730 N. Lynn Street Arlington, Va. 22209
Bookkeeper	Division of Vocational and Technical Education, Bureau of Adult Vocational and Library Programs United States Office of Education Washington, D.C. 20202
Building Trades Industry	AFL-CIO, Building & Construction Trades Dept. 815 16 Street N.W. Washington, D.C. 20006
Butcher (Meat Cutter)	American Meat Institute 59 East Van Buren Street Chicago, Ill. 60605
Chemist	Manufacturing Chemists' Association Inc. 1825 Connecticut Avenue N.W. Washington, D.C. 20009
City Manager	International City Management Association 1140 Connecticut Avenue N.W. Washington, D.C. 20036
Clothing Industry	Amalgamated Clothing Workers of America 15 Union Square New York, N.Y. 10003
Commercial Artist	National Art Ed. Association N.E.A., 1201 16 Street N.W. Washington, D.C. 20036
Cook (or Chef)	Educational Director, National Restaurant Association 153 N. Lake Shore Drive Chicago, Ill. 60610

Counselor	American School Counselor Association 1607 New Hampshire Avenue N.W. Washington, D.C. 20009
Dental Hygienist	American Dental Hygienists Association 211 East Chicago Avenue Chicago, Ill. 60611
Dental Laboratory Technician	Council on Dental Education American Dental Association 211 East Chicago Avenue Chicago, Ill. 60611
Dentist	Council on Dental Education American Dental Association 211 East Chicago Avenue Chicago, Ill. 60611
Draftsman	American Institute for Design & Drafting P.O. Box 2955 Tulsa, Oklahoma 74101
Drug Industry	Pharmaceutical Manufacturers Association 1155 15 Street N.W. Washington, D.C. 20005
Electrical Power Industry	Edison Electric Institute 750 Third Avenue New York, N.Y. 10017
Electrician	International Brotherhood of Electrical Workers 1125 15 Street N.W. Washington, D.C. 20005
Electronic Computer Operating Personnel	Data Processing Management Association 505 Busse Highway Park Ridge, Ill. 60068
Electronic Industry	Electronic Industries Association 2001 Eye Street N.W. Washington, D.C. 20006
Engineering Industry	Engineers' Council for Professional Devel- opment 345 East 47th Street New York, N.Y. 10017
FBI Special Agent	F.B.I. United States Department of Justice Washington, D.C. 20535
Federal Civil Service	U.S. Civil Service Commission

	Washington, D.C. (or your regional office)
Firefighter	Your local Civil Service Commission
Forester	Society of American Foresters 1010 16th Street N.W. Washington, D.C. 20036
Foundry Industry	American Foundrymen's Society Golf and Wolf Roads Des Plaines, Ill. 60016
Furniture Upholsterer	Upholsterers' International Union of North America 1500 N. Broad Street Philadelphia, Pa. 19121
Geologist	American Geological Institute 2201 M Street N.W. Washington, D.C. 20037
Hospital Attendant	ANA-NLN Commission on Nursing Careers American Nurses Association 10 Columbus Circle, New York, N.Y. 10019
Industrial Chemicals Industry	American Chem. Society 1155 16 Street N.W. Washington, D.C. 20036
Industrial Designer	Industrial Designers Society of America 60 West 55 Street New York, N.Y. 10019
Industrial Traffic Manager	American Society of Traffic and Transportation Inc. 22 West Madison Street Chicago, Ill. 60602
Iron & Steel Industry	American Iron & Steel Institute 150 East 42 Street New York, N.Y. 10017
Jeweler	Retail Jewelers of America 1025 Vermont Avenue N.W. Washington, D.C. 20005
Landscape Architect	American Society of Landscape Architects 2013 I Street N.W. Washington, D.C. 20006
Lawyer	Information Service, American Bar Association

	1155 East 60 Street Chicago, Ill. 60637
Librarian	American Library Association 50 East Huron Street Chicago, Ill. 60611
Machinist	International Association of Machinists & Aerospace Workers 1300 Connecticut Avenue N.W. Washington, D.C. 20036
Maritime Industry	Office of Maritime Manpower Maritime Administration U.S. Department of Commerce Washington, D.C. 20235
Marketing Research Worker	Small Business Administration Washington, D.C. 20416
Mathematician	American Mathematical Society P.O.B. 6248 Providence, R.I. 02904 (Send 25¢ for Professional Training in Mathematics)
Medical Technologist	American Society of Medical Technol- ogists Suite 1600, Hermann Professional Building Houston, Texas 77025
Meteorologist	American Meteorological Society 25 Beacon Street Boston, Mass. 02108
Mining Industry	American Institute of Mining, Metallurgi- cal & Petroleum Engineers (AIME) 345 East 47 Street New York, N.Y. 10017
Musician	American Federation of Musicians (AFL- CIO) 641 Lexington Avenue New York, N.Y. 10022
Newspaper Reporter	American Newspaper Publishers Associa- tion 750 Third Avenue New York, N.Y. 10017
Occupational Therapist	American Occupational Therapy Asso- ciation 251 Park Avenue South New York, N.Y. 10010

Oceanographer	National Oceanography Association 1900 L. Street, N.W. Washington, D.C. 20036
Operating Engineer	International Union of Operating Engineers 1125 17 Street N.W. Washington, D.C. 20036
Optician	American Board of Opticianry 821 Eggert Road Buffalo, N.Y. 14226
Optometrist	American Optometric Association 7000 Chippewa Street St. Louis, Mo. 63119
Painter	International Brotherhood of Painters & Allied Trades 1925 K Street N.W. Washington, D.C. 20006
Paper Industry	American Forest Institute 1835 K Street N.W. Washington, D.C. 20006
Personnel Worker	American Society for Personnel Administration 19 Church Street Berea, Ohio 44017
Pharmacist	American Pharmaceutical Association 2215 Constitution Avenue N.W. Washington, D.C. 20037
Photoengraver	Printing Industry of America 1730 N. Lynn Street Arlington, Va. 22209
Photographer	Professional Photographers of America Inc. 1090 Executive Way, Oak Leaf Commons Des Plaines, Ill. 60018
Physician	Council on Medical Education American Medical Association 535 N. Dearborn Street Chicago Ill. 60610
Physicist	American Institute of Physics 335 East 45 Street New York, N.Y. 10017
Pilot	Air Line Pilots' Association International 1329 E Street N.W. Washington, D.C. 20004

Plumber	National Association of Plumbing-Heating- Cooling Contractors 1016 20 Street N.W. Washington, D.C.
Podiatrist	American Podiatry Association 20 Chevy Chase Circle N.W. Washington, D.C. 20015
Police	Your local Civil Service Commission
Printing	Education Council of the Graphic Arts In. 4615 Forbes Avenue Pittsburgh, Pa. 15213
Programmer	Association for Computing Machinery 1133 Avenue of the Americas New York, N.Y. 10036
Psychologist	American Psychological Association 1200 17 Street, N.W. Washington, D.C. 20036
Public Relations Worker	The Information Center Public Relations Society of America 845 Third Avenue New York, N.Y. 10022
Railroad Industry	Association of American Railroads American Railroad Building 1920 L Street N.W. Washington, D.C. 20036
Recreation Worker	National Industrial Recreation Association 20 N. Wacker Drive Chicago, Ill. 60606
Registered Nurse	ANA-NLN Commission on Nursing Careers
Practical Nurse	American Nurses Association 10 Columbus Circle New York, N.Y. 10019
Roofer	National Roofing Contractors Association 1575 N. Harlem Avenue Oak Park, Ill. 60302
Salesperson- Automobiles	National Automobile Dealers Association 2000 K Street N.W. Washington, D.C. 20006
Salesperson Manufacturers	Sales & Marketing Exec. International Student Education Division

630 Third Avenue
New York, N.Y. 10017

Salesperson
  Real Estate   National Association of Real Estate Boards
                           Department of Education
                           155 East Superior Street
                           Chicago, Ill. 60611

Salesperson-Retail   National Retail Merchants Association
                           100 West 31 Street
                           New York, N.Y. 10001

Salesperson-Securities   New York Stock Exchange
                           11 Wall Street
                           New York, N.Y. 10005

Secretary   United Business Schools Association
                           1730 M. Street N.W.
                           Washington, D.C. 20036

Sewage Plant
  Operator   Water Pollution Control Federation
                           3900 Wisconsin Avenue N.W.
                           Washington, D.C. 20016

Singer   National Association of Schools of Music
                           One Dupont Circle N.W.
                           Washington, D.C. 20036

Skilled Worker
  (Foreman)   American Management Association
                           1315 West 50 Street
                           New York, N.Y. 10020

Social Worker   National Association of Social Workers
                           2 Park Avenue
                           New York, N.Y. 10016

Soil Scientist   Office of Personnel
                           U.S. Department of Agriculture
                           Washington, D.C. 20250

Surgical Technician   Association of Operation Room Techni-
                             cians Inc.
                           8085 East Prentice
                           The Denver Technological Center
                           Englewood, Colo. 80110

State Police   Your State Civil Service Commission

Stationary Engineer   International Union of Operating Engi-
                             neers

	1125 17 Street N.W.
	Washington, D.C. 20036
Surveyor	American Congresson Surveying & Mapping
	Woodward Building, 733 15 Street N.W.
	Washington, D.C. 20005
Systems Analyst	Data Processing Management Association
	505 Busse Highway
	Park Ridge, Ill. 60068
Teacher	American Federation of Teachers
	1012 14 Street N.W.
	Washington, D.C. 20005
Telephone Industry	Communication Workers of America
	1925 Avenue K.N.W.
	Washington, D.C. 20006
Truck Driver	American Trucking Association
	1616 P Street N.W.
	Washington, D.C. 20036
Urban Planner	American Institute of Planners
	917 15 Street N.W.
	Washington, D.C. 20005
Veterinarian	American Veterinary Med. Association
	600 South Michigan Avenue
	Chicago, Ill. 60605
Waiter or Waitress	Educational Director, National Restaurant Association
	153 N. Lake Shore Drive
	Chicago, Ill. 60610
Welder	American Welding Society
	345 East 47 Street
	New York, N.Y. 10017

APPENDIX B

THE CAREER CLUSTERS
AND RELATED OCCUPATIONS

I. AGRI-BUSINESS AND NATURAL RESOURCES

Agricultural Engineer

Animal Research Scientist

Animal Husbandman

Cooperative extension service worker

Cowboy

Farm Worker

Forester

Geophysicist

Miner

Petroleum engineer

Entomologist

Farmer—dairy, livestock, etc.

Geologist

Microbiologist

Oil refinery worker

Plant quarantine and plant pest control inspector

Plant research scientist

Rig builder

Soil conservationist

Veterinarian

Rancher

Rig builder helper

Soil scientist

Veterinary aid

II. BUSINESS AND OFFICE OCCUPATIONS

Accountant

Clerk typist

Computer programmer

Fiscal manager

Keypunch operator

Office machine operator

Office supervisor

Secretary—executive

Secretary—medical

Stenographer

Bookkeeper

Computer operator

Dealership operator

General office clerk

Machine transcriber

Office manager

Secretary

Secretary—legal

Secretary—school

Systems analyst

III. COMMUNICATION AND MEDIA

Creative writer

Darkroom worker

Editor

Illustrator

Photographer

Sign painter

Telephone lineman and cable splicer

Darkroom technician

Display technician

Electronics engineer

Layout men

Reporter

Telephone installer

TV and radio announcer TV and radio engineer
TV and radio program director TV and radio repair technician

IV. CONSTRUCTION

Architect—commercial Architect—industrial
Architect—landscape Architect—residential
Bricklayer Carpenter
Cement mason Construction laborer
Electrician Elevator constructors
Engineer—civil Engineer—electrical
Engineer—mechanical Floor covering installer
Glazier Iron worker
Lather Marble setter
Metal worker Operating engineer (crane opera-
  tor)

Painter Paper hanger
Plasterer Plumber and pipefitter
Roofer Sheet metal worker
Stonemason

V. CONSUMER AND HOME MAKING

Cleaner Chef
Laundry worker Cook
Presser
Clothing Assembler Dietician
Clothing—cutter Food demonstrator
Clothing designer Food journalist
Clothing inspector Food processor
Clothing machine operator Food purchaser
Clothing pattern maker Food tester
Clothing presser Home economist
Clothing weaver
Consumer counselor Waiter
Food service industry worker

  Furniture maker
Furniture refinisher Home management counselor
Household day worker Housekeeper
Interior decorator Product demonstrator
Upholsterer

VI. ENVIRONMENT

Air analyst Industrial pollution controller
Anti-pollution law enforcer
Bacteriologist Landscape Architect
Conservationist Marine biologist

Engine emission inspector
Exterminator

Farmer
Florist
Game warden
Gardener
Hydroponic plant culturist

Meteorologist
Mine and dump restoration controller
Pollution control engineer
Pollution regulation enforcer
Sanitation men
Soil analyst
Urban planner
Water analyst

VII. FINE ARTS AND HUMANITIES

Actor—film
Actor—radio
Actor—television
Artist manager
Cameraman
Costume designer
Costume maker
Creative writer—essay
Creative writer—novel
Creative writer—plays
Creative writer—poet
Creative writer—short stories
Dancer
Fashion designer
Film editor
Film processor
Film producer

Foreign language broadcaster
Foreign language interpreter
Foreign language teacher
Foreign language writer
Illustrator
Industrial designer
Music composer
Painter
Printmaker
Recording technician
Sculptor
Stage lighter
Stage lighting designer
Stage manager
Stage set constructor
Stage set designer
Tape editor
Tape producer

VIII. HEALTH SERVICE OCCUPATIONS

Biochemist
Biophysicist
Chiropractor
Dental assistant
Dental hygienist
Dental laboratory technician
Dentist
Dietician
Electrocardiographic technician
Electroencephalographic technician
Hospital administrator
Inhalation therapist
Licensed practical nurse

Medical record librarian
Occupational therapist
Occupational therapy assistant
Optometric assistant
Optometrist
Osteopathic physician
Pharmacist
Physical therapist

Physical therapy assistant

Physican
Podiatrist
Radiologic technologist (X-ray technician)

Medical assistant
Medical illustrator
Medical laboratory worker
Medical photographer

Registered nurse
Sanitarian
Speech pathologist
Surgical technician
Veterinarian

IX. HOSPITALITY AND RECREATION

Bellmen and bell captain
Bus driver
Chef
Church group
Coach
Cook
Front office clerk
Hotel or motel housekeeper and assistant
Hotel or motel manager and assistant
Movie projectionist
Museum curator
Museum guard
Park maintenance worker
Park planner

Park ranger
Playground supervisor
Pre-school and day-care center personnel
Professional athlete
Senior citizen center supervisor
Sports director
Teacher—adult education or after-school activities
Theatre operator
Theatre ushers
Tour guide
Travel agent
Waiter
Waitress

X. MANUFACTURING

Assembly line operator
Distributor
Equipment producer-electro-mechanical
Equipment producer—foundry
Equipment producer—machine
Industrial engineer
Industrial psychologist
Personnel director
Plant manager
Plant supervisor
Product designer

Product developer
Product inspector
Product packager
Product promoter
Product promotion research
Product storer
Product tester
Product transporter
Retailer
Wholesaler

XI. MARINE SCIENCE OCCUPATIONS

Deep sea diver
Fish hatching and raising
Fish or shellfish culture
Life guard
Marine animal researcher
Marine biological laboratory worker

Ocean mineral explorer
Offshore mineral driller
Offshore pipe system constructor
Scuba diver
Seafood Inspector

Seafood processor

Marine plant grower
Marine plant researcher
Ocean current and water re-
searcher
Ocean fishing boat operator
Oceanographic mapper

Sport fishing processor
Underwater construction worker

Underwater demolition worker
Underwater engineering researcher
Underwater salvage operator

XII. PERSONAL SERVICES OCCUPATIONS

Animal boarder
Animal trainer
Bartender
Chef
Dry cleaner

Guard
Hair stylist
Makeup technician
Private household worker
Watchman

Animal groomer
Barber
Building custodian
Cook
Figure analyst and weight coun-
selor
Hairdresser
Laundry worker
Masseur
Waiter
Wig maker

XIII. PUBLIC SERVICE OCCUPATIONS

Agricultural advisors
Building inspector
Counselor—rehabilitation
Elected officials
Engineers
Hospital workers
Internal Revenue Service
Labor inspectors
Licensers
Marine corps
Plant and animal inspectors
Port authority workers
Public recorders

Research workers
Teachers

Army
Coast guard
Customs officials
Employment counselors
Firemen
Immigration inspectors
Judges
Librarians
Maintenance workers
Navy
Policemen—city or state
Post office workers
Registrars and licensers of cars
and drivers
Sanitation men
Traffic controllers

XIV. TRANSPORTATION

Bus drivers
Airline dispatchers
Clerks
Ground radio operators and
teletypists
Stewards and stewardesses
Merchant mariner officers

Aircraft mechanics
Air traffic controllers
Flight engineers

Pilots
Traffic agents
Unlicensed merchant seamen

Railroad brakemen	Clerks
Conductors	Locomotive engineers
Locomotive firemen	Signal workers
Station agents	Telegraphers, telephoners, tower-men
Track workers	Taxi drivers
Truck drivers—local	Over-the-road drivers (trucks)
Truck mechanics	Automobile mechanics

APPENDIX C

SELECTED REFERENCES ON
CAREER EDUCATION
CENTER FOR VOCATIONAL
AND TECHNICAL EDUCATION—Ohio State U.

The following list of selected references contains some significant documents currently available on "Career Education." These references should prove useful to educators for planning, implementing, and operating career education programs. For additional information, refer to *Research in Education* (RIE), *Abstracts of Reserach Materials in Vocational and Technical Education* (ARM), *Abstracts of Instructional Materials in Vocational and Technical Education* (AIM), and *Current Index to Journals in Education* (CIJE). Instructions for ordering ERIC documents are attached to this reference list.

Adams, Dewey Allen. *Review and Synthesis of Research Concerning Adult Vocational and Technical Education.* Information Series No. 58. Columbus: The Center for Vocational and Technical Education, The Ohio State University. April, 1972. 76 pp. ED 064 469 MF $0.65 HC $3.29. Also available from the Government Printing Office, Washington, D.C. 20402.

American Vocational Association. "Career Education—Is It a Fad or a Major Development?" *American Vocational Journal.* Vol. 47, No. 3 (March, 1972), entire issue.

Bailey, L.J., ed. *Facilitating Career Development: An Annotated Bibliography.* Final Report. Springfield: Division of Vocational and Technical Education, Illinois State Board of Vocational Education and Rehabilitation; and Carbondale: Southern Illinois University. July, 1970. 137 pp. ED 042 217 MF $0.65 HC $6.58.

Banathy, Bela H., and Peterson, Robert M. "Employer Based Career Education (EBCE)—A Model Developed at the Far West Laboratory for Educational Research and Development." Paper presented at the 1972 Annual Meeting of the American Educational Research Association, Chicago, Illinois, April 4, 1972. Complete text 49 pp. ED 062 539 MF $0.65 HC $3.29.

Bottoms, Gene. *Career Development Education K Through Post*

Secondary and Adult Education. Mimeograph. Atlanta: Division of Vocational Education, Georgia State Department of Education. n.d. 50 pp. Ed 062 580 MF $0.65 HC $3.29.

Bottoms, Gene. *Orientation to New Concepts and Programs of Career Orientation and Occupational Education for Students in Rural Areas.* Raleigh: Center for Occupational Education, North Carolina State University. December, 1970. 142 pp. ED 057 966 MF $0.65 HC $6.58.

Bottoms, Gene, and Mathny, Kenneth B. "Occupational Guidance, Counseling, and Job Placement for Junior High and Secondary School Youth." Paper presented at the 1969 National Conference on Exemplary Programs and Projects. (Atlanta, Georgia, March 12-14, 1969). 17 pp. Complete text 255 pp. VT 008 896, MF available in VT-ERIC Set ED 045 860.

Budke, Wesley E. *Review and Synthesis of Information on Occupational Exploration.* Information Series No. 34. Columbus: The Center for Vocational and Technical Education, The Ohio State University. 1971. 93 pp. ED 056 165 MF $0.65 HC $3.29. Also available from the Government Printing Office, Stock No. 1780-0763, $0.55.

Burchill, George W. "Work-Experience Programs for Secondary Youth." Paper presented at the National Conference on Exemplary Programs and Projects—1968 Amendments to the Vocational Education Act. (Atlanta, Georgia, March 12-14, 1969). 28 pp. Complete text 255 pp. VT 008 896, MF available in VT-ERIC Set Ed 045 860.

Burkett, Lowell A. "AVA Formulates Position on Career Education." *American Vocational Journal.* Vol. 47, No. 1 (January, 1972), pp. 9-14.

Bush, Donald O., et al. *Between Education and the World of Work: The Image of the World of Work.* Occupational Education Program. Greeley, CO: Rocky Mountain Educational Laboratory, Inc. February, 1969. 122 pp. ED 032 582 MF $0.65 HC $6.58.

Butler, Cornelius F. "The Home-Community Based Model (Model Three) of the U.S. Office of Education's Career Education Research and Development Program—A Synopsis." Papers presented at the 1972 Annual Meeting of the American Educational Research Association (Chicago, Illinois, April 4, 1972). Complete text 49 pp. ED 062 539 MF $0.65 HC $3.29.

Butler, Roy L., and York, Edwin G. *What School Administrators Should Know About Cooperative Vocational Education.* Information Series No. 37. Columbus: The Center for Vocational and Technical Education, The Ohio State University. August, 1971. 18 pp. ED 057 180 MF $0.65 HC $3.29.

Campbell, Robert E. "A Procedural Model for Upgrading Career Guidance Programs." *American Vocational Journal.* Vol. 47, No. 1 (January, 1972), pp. 101-103.

Campbell, Robert E. and Vetter, Louise. *Career Guidance: An Overview of Alternative Approaches.* Information Series No. 45. Columbus: The Center for Vocational and Technical Education, The Ohio State University. August, 1971. 21 pp. ED 057 183 MF $0.65 HC $3.29.

Campbell, Robert E., et al. *The Systems Approach: An Emerging Behavioral Model for Vocational Guidance.* A Summary Report. Research and Development Series No. 45. Columbus: The Center for Vocational and Technical Education, The Ohio State University. January, 1971. 33 pp. ED 047 127 MF $0.65 HC $3.29.

Career Education Washington, D.C.: U.S. Government Printing Office. 1971. 16 pp. Pamphlet. Order No. HE 5.280:80075, $0.20.

"Career Education: A Model for Implementation." *Business Education Forum.* Vol. 25, No. 8 (May, 1971), pp. 3-5.

Dunn. C.J., and Payne, Bill F. *World of Work: Occupational-Vocational Guidance in the Elementary Grades; A Handbook for Teachers and Counselors.* Dallas: The Leslie Press. 1971. 200 pp.

Elliot, Ian. "Occupation Orientation Means Work for You." *Grade Teacher.* Vol. 88, No. 8 (April, 1971), pp. 60-65.

Gibson, Robert L. *Career Development in the Elementary School.* Columbus, OH: Charles E. Merrill Publishing Company. 1972. 90 pp. ED 064 478, document not available from EDRS. Available from Charles E. Merrill Publishing Company, Columbus, Ohio ($1.95).

Goldhammer, Keith, and Taylor, Robert E. *Career Education: Perspective and Promise.* Columbus, OH: Charles E. Merrill Publishing Company. 1972. 300 pp. ED 064 517, document not available from EDRS. Available from Charles E. Merrill Publishing Company, Columbus, Ohio ($5.94).

Granger, Kolene M. *Junior High Career Guidance Curriculum—Student-Centered Occupational Preparation and Exploration (SCOPE).* Teacher Supplement. Salt Lake City: Utah Board of Education. June, 1972. 351 pp. VT 016 136, see AIM Vol. 5, No. 4.

Gysbers, Norman C. "Elements of a Model for Promoting Career Development in Elementary and Junior High School." Papers presented at the 1969 National Conference on Exemplary Programs and Projects–1968 Amendments to the Vocational Education Act. (Atlanta, Georgia, March 12-14, 1969). 26 pp. Complete text 255 pp. VT 008 806, MF available in VT-ERIC Set 045 860.

Gysbers, Norman C. and Pritchard, David H., eds. *National Conference on Guidance, Counseling, and Placement in Career Development and Educational-Occupational Decision Making, Proceedings* (University of Missouri, Columbia, Oct. 20-24, 1969). Washington, D.C.: U.S. Office of Education. October, 1969. 109 pp. ED 041 143 MF $0.65 HC $6.58.

Hansen, Lorraine S., et al. *Career Guidance Practices in School and Community*. Ann Arbor, MI: ERIC Clearinghouse on Counseling and Personnel Services. 1970. 200 pp. ED 037 595 MF $0.65 HC $6.58.

Heilman, Cas F., and Gardner, Richard E. *Exploration in Careers Education*. Careers Oriented Relevant Education. Springfield, OR: Springfield Public Schools; and Corvallis: School of Education, Oregon State University. 1972. 205 pp. VT 016 008, see AIM Vol. 6. No. 1.

Herr, Edwin L. *Decision-Making and Vocational Development*. Boston, MA: Houghton-Mifflin Company, 1970.

Herr, Edwin L. *Review and Synthesis of Foundations for Career Education*. Information Series No. 61. Columbus: The Center for Vocational and Technical Education, The Ohio State University. 1972. 85 pp. ED 059 402 MF $0.65 HC $3.29. Also available from the Government Printing Office, Washington, D.C. 20402.

Herr, Edwin L. "Unifiying An Entire System of Education Around a Career Development Theme." Papers presented at the 1969 National Conference on Exemplary Programs and Projects–1968 Amendments to the Vocational Education Act. (Atlanta, Georgia, March 12-14, 1969). 36 pp. Complete text 255 pp. VT 008 896, MF available in VT-ERIC Set ED 045 860.

Herr, Edwin L. and Cramer, Stanley H. *Vocational Guidance and Career Development in the Schools: Toward a Systems Approach*. Boston, MA: Houghton-Mifflin Company, 1972.

Hoyt, Kenneth B., et al. *Career Education: What It Is and How to Do It*. Salt Lake City, UT: Olympus Publishing Company, 1972. 190 pp.

Introducing Career Education to Teachers: A Handbook for Consultants, Workshop Leaders, and Teacher Educators. De Kalb: Northern Illinois University; and Springfield: Vocational and

Technical Education Division, Illinois State Board of Vocational Education and Rehabilitation. April, 1972. 110 pp. VT 016 637, see AIM Vol. 6, No. 1.

Kunzman, Leonard E. *Career Education in Oregon.* A Statement In Improvement of Vocational Instruction in Oregon Schools. Salem: Oregon State Board of Education. August 1, 1970. 11 pp. VT 011 799, MF available in VT-ERIC Set ED 051 432.

Lamar, Carl. "Implications for Meeting the Needs of People." *American Vocational Journal.* Vol. 46, No. 4 (April, 1971), pp. 31-35.

Law, Gordon F., ed. *Contemporary Concepts in Vocational Education.* The First Yearbook of the American Vocational Association. Washington, D.C.: the American Vocational Association, Inc., 1510 H Street, N.W. 1971. 435 pp.

Laws, Lee. *Elementary Guide for Career Development; Grades 1-6.* Austin, TX: Education Service Center. 1970.

"Marland on Career Education." Reprinted from *American Education.* (November, 1971). Washington, D.C.: The Government Printing Office, Order No. HE 5.280:80076, $0.10.

Marland, Sidney P., Jr. "Career Education: More than a Name." Speech presented to the Meeting of the State Directors of Vocational Education (Annual, Washington, D.C., May 4, 1971). 1971. 14 pp. ED 050 295 MF $0.65 HC $3.29.

Marland, Sidney P., Jr. "Career Education Now." Presentation at the National Association of Secondary School Principals (Houston, Texas, January 23, 1971). January, 1971. 15 pp. ED 048 480 MF $0.65 HC $3.29.

Martin, Ann. *The Theory and Practice of Communicating Educational and Vocational Information.* Series IV: Career Information and Development; Guidance Monograph Series. Boston: Houghton Mifflin Co. 1971. 80 pp.

Matheny, Kenneth B. "The Role of the Middle School in Career Development." *American Vocational Journal.* Vol. 44, No. 9 (December 1969), pp. 18-21.

Miller, Aaron J. "Strategies for Implementing Career Education: A School Based Model." *Career Education:* Papers presented at the 1972 Annual Meeting of the American Educational Research Association (Chicago, Illinois, April 4, 1972). Complete text 49 pp. ED 062 539 MF $0.65 HC $3.29.

Minelli, Ernest L. *Innovative Programs in Industrial Arts,* Washington, D.C.: American Vocational Association, 1510 H Street, N.W. May, 1970. 36 pp. ED 043 734 MF $0.65 HC $3.29.

Moore, Allen B., *Abstracts of Instructional Materials for Career Education.* Bibliography Series No. 15. Columbus: The Center for Vocational and Technical Education, The Ohio State University, 1972. 125 pp. VT 016 524, see February 1973 RIE. Document not available from EDRS. Available from The Center for Vocational and Technical Education, The Ohio State University, 1960 Kenny Road, Columbus, Ohio 43210, $2.25.

Moore, Allen B., and King, Sue J. *Problem Areas in Occupational Education for the 1970's.* Raleigh: The Center for Occupational Education, North Carolina State University. 1972. 26 pp. ED 062 544 MF $0.65 HC $3.29.

Moore, Samuel A., II. *Strategies for Implementing Exemplary Programs and Projects in Order to Make Maximum Change in the Educational Process.* East Lansing: Michigan State University. n.d. 16 pp. VT 013 723, MF available in VT-ERIC Set ED 062 579.

Morgan, Robert L., et al., eds. *Synopses of Selected Career Education Programs: A National Overview of Career Education.* Raleigh: The Center for Occupational Education, North Carolina State University. April, 1972. 79 pp. ED 063 461 MF $0.65 HC $3.29.

Morgan, Robert L. *The Plan for Implementation of an Exemplary Occupational Education Program in a Rural Community.* Raleigh: The Center for Occupational Education, North Carolina State University. 1970. 32 pp. ED 050 296 MF $0.65 HC $3.29.

Olympus Research Corporation. *Career Education: A Handbook for Implementation.* Salt Lake City, UT: Olympus Research Corporation; and Baltimore: Maryland State Department of Education. February, 1972. 102 pp. ED 062 521 MF $0.65 HC $6.58.

Palo Alto Educational Systems, Inc. *A First Step Toward Career Education.* Volume I. Appendices—Volume II. Palo Alto , AZ: Palo Alto Educational Systems, Inc. 1972. 251 pp. ED 060 224 MF $0.65 HC $9.87.

Peterson, Marla. "Occupacs for Hands-On Learning." *American Vocational Journal.* Vol. 47, No. 1 (January, 1972), pp. 40-41.

Rhodes, James A. *Vocational Education and Guidance: A System for the Seventies.* Columbus, OH: Charles E. Merrill Publishing Company. 1970.

Spires, Jerald V., and McMahon, Edward J. *Career Education.* Elementary School Teachers' Guide to Ideas. Career Awareness, Grades 1-6. Portland OR: David Douglas Public Schools; and Washington, D.C.: U.S. Office of Education. 1972. 153 pp. VT 015 365, see AIM Vol. 5, No. 4.

Swanson, Gordon I. "Facts and Fantasies of Career Education." *Career Education:* Papers presented at the 1972 Annual Meeting of the American Educational Research Association (Chicago, Illinois, April 4, 1972). Complete text 49 pp. ED 062 539 MF $0.65 HC $3.29.

Tennyson, W. Wesley. "Career Development." *Review of Educational Research.* Vol. 38, No. 4 (October, 1968), pp. 346-366.

Tennyson, W. Wesley. "Career Development: Who's Responsible?" *American Vocational Journal.* Vol. 46, No. 3 (March, 1971), pp. 54-58.

Thomas, Hollie B., and Thomas, Susan B. "Development of a Career Interest Inventory." Presentation at the Annual Convention of the National Council for Measurement in Education (Chicago, Illinois, 1972). East Lansing: National Council on Measurement in Education, Office of Evaluation Services, Michigan State University. 1971. 13 pp. VT 016 014, see ARM Vol. 6, No. 1.

Tuckman, Bruce W. *An Age-Graded Model for Career Development Education.* Trenton: Research Coordinating Unit, Division of Vocational Education, New Jersey State Department of Education. December, 1971. 43 pp. ED 060 180 MF $0.65 HC $3.29.

Turnbull, William W., chrm. *Proceedings of the Conferences on Career Education* (Beverly Hills, CA; and Washington, D.C.: May 1972). Princeton, NJ: Educational Testing Service. 1972. 103 pp.

U.S. Office of Education. *Abstacts of Exemplary Projects in Vocational Education.* Washington, DC: Division of Vocational and Technical Education, U.S. Office of Education. November, 1971. 124 pp. ED 060 189 MF $0.65 HC $6.58.

U.S. Office of Education. *Summary of the Secretary's Regional Conferences on Vocational Education.* Region VI Conference, Dallas, Texas, April 29-30, 1971. Washington, DC: U.S. Office of Education, Department of Health, Education, and Welfare. 1971.

Wenig, Robert E., and Wolansky, William D. *Review and Synthesis of Literature on Job Training in Industry.* Information Series No. 62. Columbus: The Center for Vocational and Technical Education, The Ohio State University. June, 1972. 72 pp. ED 062 514 MF $0.65 HC $3.29. Also available from the Government Printing Office, Washington, D.C. 20402.

Worthington, Robert M. *Career Education and the Community Junior College.* Presentation at the National Seminar for State Directors of Community-Junior Colleges (Columbus, Ohio,

January 10, 1972). January 10, 1972. 12 pp. VT 016 518, see ARM Vol. 6, No. 1.

Worthington, Robert M. *Comprehensive Personnel Development for Career Education.* Presentation at the Annual Leadership Development Seminar for State Directors of Vocational Education (4th, Las Vegas, Nevada, September 15, 1972). Washington, DC: Bureau of Adult, Vocational, and Technical Education, U.S. Office of Education. September 15, 1971. 38 pp. VT 016 575, see ARM Vol. 6, No. 1.

Worthington, Robert M. *Technical Education, Careers Unlimited.* Presentation before the National Technical Education Clinic (Fort Worth, Texas, March 15, 1972). Washington, D.C.: Bureau of Adult, Vocational, and Technical Education, U.S. Office of Education. March 15, 1972. 25 pp. VT 016 574, see ARM Vol. 6, No. 1.

Index

INDEX